The Bread of Life

A Study of the Life of Christ

PART I

by

Greg Litmer

truth
BOOKS

WWW.TRUTHBOOKS.NET

ISBN 10: 1-58427-344-5

ISBN 13: 978-1-58427-3448

truth
BOOKS

WWW.TRUTHBOOKS.NET

Guardian of Truth Foundation
C E I Bookstore
220 South Marion
Athens, AL 35611
Truthbooks.net
1-855-492-6657

Table of Contents

1

The Prologue
(Luke 1:1-4)

The early years of the church apparently saw many attempts by various individuals to produce a written record of the acts and words of Jesus. Luke saw the need for an account of the life of the Lord that would be accurate and complete. This would be particularly true as the Lord's church grew, the disciples multiplied, and the eyewitnesses of the events were slowly dying. So, under the inspiration of the Holy Spirit, Luke wrote such an account.

Luke went to those who from the beginning were eyewitnesses and made a careful investigation of all things from the beginning. His purpose was to present to Theophilus a record arranged in an orderly fashion.

> We stand at the threshold of the most important and exciting study into which a man can enter – the study of the life of Christ. Jesus, the central figure of all of history, lies before us. We will focus on the four gospel accounts and attempt to arrange them in as chronological a fashion as possible.

What of "Theophilus"? The name is derived from two Greek words and means "friend of God." This indicates that Theophilus was probably a Greek and a Christian. That he was called "most excellent" gives us reason to believe that he held a high position of some sort. Thus, the Gospel of Luke was written to satisfy the needs of an educated individual. It is obvious that the book was written for a Greek audience, yet beneficial to all people of all time.

The Pre-existence of Christ and the Incarnation (John 1:1-18)

When studying the life of Christ we must go back before the beginning. We might ask, "What beginning?" The answer is the beginning of creation, the beginning of time. John starts his gospel with the same phrase used by Moses in Genesis 1:1, "In the beginning."

At the "beginning," the Word already existed. What is the significance of that truth?

The essential elements of time are a beginning and an ending. This is true of a second, a year, or a millennium. Time is that which is between. That which was before creation had an ending at creation, but it had no beginning – it is timeless, eternal. That which will be after the judgment will have a beginning, but it will have no ending. It will be timeless, eternal (Foster, *Studies in the Life of Christ,* 223)

The Word had no beginning, existed at the beginning of creation and therefore was not created. The Word is eternal. Not only is the Word eternal, the Word was "with God." This shows us that the Word was co-existent with God. It shows the separate personality of the Word and God, as well as their inseparable relationship.

The Word "was God," not a god; nor "the" God; the Word was God – absolute Deity. Thus, the Word was God in His nature and being, possessing all of the power and attributes of Deity. Consider the title Word, or *Logos*, as it relates to Jesus. If the nature of a word is considered it helps to understand its significance when used of Christ. A word does essentially two things. It expresses a thought and reveals that thought to others.

The Greek for "all things" in v. 3 emphasizes all things, one by one, separate and particular. Consider Colossians 1:16-17. Jesus was the agent of creation. In Him was the very essence of life and through His life, light was given to men. It was the light that illumines and appeals to reason, promoting a response. Yet, as the light came into the world, the darkness (moral darkness) did not understand it. From the moment this light entered into the world there was conflict between it and the darkness. John the Baptist was a messenger divinely sent into the world with a divine message. His job was to bear witness to the light, to announce His coming.

Jesus was in the world, perhaps in the sense of being its Creator and the One who holds all things together. When He came unto His own, probably referring to the Jews, but possibly referring to all men as all were created by Him, they rejected Him. However, not all reacted to Jesus in such a way. Some received Him, defined as "those who believe in His name." Isn't it interesting that verse 12 tells us that those who believed were said to have been given "the right to become children of God," not that they were children of God already merely on the basis of belief?

In verse 14 a truth marvelous to contemplate is set forth. God was made flesh and tabernacled among men. This is known as the Incarnation. Here was Deity in the flesh; visible, able to be touched and heard. He was walking the very streets that He had created. The Incarnation was absolutely unique. He was "the only begotten of the Father." Nothing like it had occurred before and nothing like it has occurred since. If we want to see Deity, look to Jesus. Colossians 1:19 says, "For it was the Father's good pleasure for all the fullness to dwell in Him." Colossians 2:9 tells us, "For in Him all the fullness of Deity dwells in bodily form."

The Genealogies (Matt. 1:1-17; Luke 3:23-28)

Matthew's genealogy is the shorter of the two. It goes from Abraham forward 42 generations ending with "Joseph the husband of Mary, by whom was born Jesus, who is called Christ." It is divided into 3 groups of 14 each. The first group is from Abraham to David, the second from David to the Babylonian Captivity, and the third is from the Captivity to Jesus. Matthew was not only demonstrating the connection of Jesus to David, he was also supplying somewhat of a history lesson. He was connecting the ancestry of Jesus to David and tracing the rise, fall, and rise again of the house of David.

The genealogy in Luke is different from the one in Matthew. It runs backwards from Jesus to Adam, 76 generations. There are differences in some of the names presented. I believe these differences are explained by understanding what each writer was accomplishing. It seems most plausible to me that Joseph was the son-in-law of Heli, and that Luke is actually tracing the line of Mary while Matthew was tracing the line of Joseph. Thus, Matthew was giving the legal line of descent while Luke was giving the biological, or natural, line of descent. The point is, the Old Testament prophets declared that the One who was to come would be of the line of David. He has come, and these genealogies prove His ancestry.

Questions

1. What motivated Luke to produce a written record of Jesus' life and words?
   _____

2. How was Luke's account of the gospel different from other writers' accounts? _____
   _____

3. What do we know of Theophilus? _____
   _____

4. Which of the following is (are) true of Luke's account?
   a. It was written for the Jewish population only. _____
   b. It was written by a Greek for the Greeks. _____
   c. It was written in chronological order. _____
   d. It was written as the most personal account of the gospels. _____

5. Which came first, God or the Word? _____

6. Explain why the expression, "Where will you *spend* eternity?" is ineffectual.
   _____

7 Why did John the Baptist come? _____
   _____

8. Define "tabernacle." Explain how God came to "tabernacle among men."
   _____

9. Which of the following statements is/are TRUE about light?
   a. Light can coexist with darkness. _____
   b. Jesus is the essence of light. _____
   c. Light was given to all men through the gospel as recorded by John. ___
   d. Darkness extended throughout the world when Jesus died. _____

10. Explain how "those who believed" had the right to become children of God. _____
    _____

11. Explain how there are no inconsistencies in the genealogies of Matthew and Luke, although they appear to be different. _____
    _____

12. Find Old Testament prophecies that spoke of the lineage of Christ.
    _____

Notes

2 The Birth of John Announced

(Luke 1:5-25)

Augustus Caesar ruled the Roman Empire from 27 B.C. to A.D. 14. He was ruling when John and Jesus were born.

The marvelous birth of Jesus begins to unfold in the days of Herod the Great, the son of Antipater, founder of the Herodian line. This Herod ruled from 37 to 4 B.C. The emperor in Rome at the time was Octavian, Caesar Augustus. This is important as it places the events surrounding Christ in the days of the fourth world empire, Rome, as prophesied in Daniel 2.

There was a priest, Zacharias, described as "of the division of Abijah." When the number of priests became so numerous that they could not all administer at the altar at one time, David divided them into 24 courses, or divisions. Each of these courses would officiate for one week (1 Chron. 23:16; 24:1-31). Abijah was the eighth in order. Zacharias' wife, Elizabeth, was a descendant of Aaron; and both Zacharias and Elizabeth are described as exemplary in their conduct and "advanced in years." Elizabeth was barren.

As Zacharias was offering incense at the altar of incense, located just outside of the double veil that separated the Holy Place from the Most Holy Place, the Holy of Holies, the angel Gabriel appeared to him. The troubled and fearful reaction of Zacharias would have been quite natural. Gabriel informed Zacharias that the prayer of both him and Elizabeth had been heard. A son would be born to them. He would be an unusual child. He would be filled with the Holy Spirit from his mother's womb. He would be a Nazarite (Num. 6:1-8). He would "turn back many of the sons of Israel to the Lord their God" as he came in "in the spirit and power of Elijah" (Mal. 4:5), acting as a forerunner of Him who was to come (Mal. 3:1). Because of the incredible nature of the things he was being told, Zacharias requested a sign, proof that it was going to come to pass. The sign he was given was to be struck dumb, unable to speak, until the things promised occurred. After the completion of his course, Zacharias returned to his home in the hill country of Judea, and Elizabeth conceived.

The Birth of Jesus Announced (Luke 1:26-38)

In the sixth month after Elizabeth's conception the angel Gabriel was sent by God with a divine message. He was sent to Nazareth of Galilee, where he appeared to a young virgin named Mary who was espoused to a man named

Joseph. Both Mary and Joseph were of the house of David. Mary would bear a son whose named would be called Jesus. He would be great, called the Son of the Most High, be given the throne of David, and reign over the house of Jacob forever, His kingdom knowing no end. How could this happen? She was engaged to Joseph but not yet married. An engagement among the Jews generally lasted ten to twelve months and was a binding contract to marry. Any unfaithfulness during this time was considered adultery. What would happen to her would happen through the power of the Holy Spirit. Her child would have no earthly father. This would be a miraculous conception. Perhaps as a sign of the truthfulness of the promise, Mary was told that her relative, Elizabeth, had conceived in her old age, for nothing is impossible with God.

Mary Visits Elizabeth (Luke 1:39-56)

Mary quickly made her way into the hill country of Judea to the home of Zacharias and Elizabeth. Upon hearing the salutation of Mary, the babe in Elizabeth's womb, John, leaped or started. Elizabeth, filled with the Holy Spirit, announced the unique position Mary occupied among woman. She would be the mother of her Lord. An important point to make here is that Mary had everything to do with the physical aspect of Jesus; she had nothing to do with His divinity. To refer to Mary as the Mother of God implies something that is simply not true.

Mary's statement or poem of praise is known as the Magnificat. This is the Latin word with which it begins and means "does magnify." It is filled with Old Testament references and magnifies the name of God. As the promised arrival of the Messiah was soon to occur, what better way than in praise of the One who so loved the world as to send His only begotten Son to die for all of mankind?

The Birth of John (Luke 1:57-80)

Elizabeth reached full term and delivered her promised son. In compliance with Genesis 17:10-12, the child was circumcised on the eighth day. Those involved were going to name him Zacharias; however, Elizabeth intervened and gave him the name John. To make certain that John was to be the name, it was asked of Zacharias by signs if this was to be the case. When he wrote on a tablet, "His name is John," his mouth was immediately opened and his tongue loosed. Filled with the Holy Spirit, Zacharias proclaimed a two-part prophecy. First, God had looked upon His people, knew their need, and was taking steps to redeem them. Using a horn, a symbol of power, he spoke of the One who was yet in the womb of His mother. He would be of the house of David and would bring the power of salvation to His people. All that was taking place had been spoken by the prophets. Zacharias referred to the oath made to Abraham, bringing to mind Genesis 22:16-18. Surely Abraham's posterity was being blessed. The promises were being fulfilled concerning the coming of the Messiah. Secondly, John would act as a spokesman for God, preparing the way for the Lord. He would announce that the kingdom of heaven was at hand. He would announce salvation through the remission of sins. Only through this salvation, made actual by the death, burial, and resurrection of Jesus, could man come to know true mercy, light and peace.

The young man John now steps into obscurity for a time. He would reside in the deserts of Judea, becoming strong in spirit, acquiring the character necessary to step into public and shake the people from their spiritual lethargy.

Notes

The Announcement to Joseph of the Impending Birth of Jesus (Matthew 1:18:25)

After her visit with Elizabeth, Mary returned home, and the fact that she was with Child was evident. The only explanation was that the Child was conceived through the Holy Spirit, for that is what the angel Gabriel told her. What was the situation in which Mary found herself? Deuteronomy 22:23-24 indicates that Mary would have been viewed as being guilty of adultery and could have been put to death. However, Joseph was a righteous man with the passage indicating that he was a man of tender heart with true feelings for Mary. He determined to put her away secretly. Deuteronomy 24:1 would be applicable here.

While he was contemplating his course of action, Joseph was visited by an angel of the Lord in a dream. He received assurance that corroborated what Mary had apparently told him. The Child she was carrying was of the Holy Spirit. He would be called Jesus, that is, Savior – derived from the verb signifying to save.

Much attention has been paid to the Hebrew word translated "virgin" in Isaiah 7:14. Many contend that "virgin" is an incorrect translation and that it should be rendered "young woman." The word itself is *almah*.

The word occurs in the following instances and in each obviously designates an unmarried woman and a true virgin – Psalm 68:15, Exodus 2:8, Proverbs 30:19. Genesis 24:43, Song of Solomon 1:3, 6:8, and Isaiah 7:14 (Guy N. Woods, *The Living Messages of the Books of the Old Testament*, 261).

Being thus assured, Joseph took Mary to wife and did not consummate the marriage until after the birth of the Lord.

The Birth of the Savior (Matt. 2:1; Luke 1:1-7)

It came to pass in the days surrounding the birth of Jesus that a decree came forth from the emperor of Rome, Octavian, Caesar Augustus, that a census be taken of all the world under Roman rule. The purpose of such an enrollment would be to assist in the work of taxation and also to determine how many were subject to military service. Octavian ruled in Rome from 31 B.C. to A.D. 15. At this time, Quirinius was governor of Syria. Roman custom was for each person to be enrolled in their place of residence. However, the Jews went to be enrolled in their ancestral homes.

Joseph and Mary, both of the lineage of David, made their way to Bethlehem, the city of David, to be enrolled. While in the city of Bethlehem, in the most humble circumstances imaginable, Jesus was born. The Lord was born in a stable for there was no room for Him in an inn, undoubtedly due to the large number of people in the city for the census. His first bed was a manger. Was there significance to Bethlehem as His birthplace? It had been prophesied in Micah 5:2.

The Shepherds and Angels (Luke 2:8-20)

In the hill country around Bethlehem shepherds were watching over their sheep by night. Suddenly an angel of the Lord appeared to them and there was great brightness as the glory of the Lord shone around them. Why shepherds? I believe it was to demonstrate that the work of the Lord was for all men, from the least to the greatest; there is no class distinction in the love of God and the availability of salvation. It was announced to them, "Today in the city of David there has been born for you a Savior, who is Christ the Lord." They were given a sign by which they could recognize Him. They would find the baby wrapped in cloths and lying in a manger. A multitude of the heavenly host appeared praising God.

With haste the shepherds made their way to Bethlehem to see the thing that the angel had said. They found Mary, Joseph, and the child Jesus lying in a manger just as they had been told. With that, these lowly men became the first preachers of Jesus. They made known what had been told to them. How could Mary do anything else but ponder these things in her heart?

Questions

1. Explain what each verse prophesied of John the Baptist.
   a. Numbers 6:1-8 _____
   b. Malachi 3:1 _____
   c. Malachi 4:5 _____
2. After hearing the angel Gabriel's message, Zacharias became speechless. . .
   a. out of shock that Elizabeth was to have a child.
   b. as a sign to validate what he had heard.
   c. as part of his vow to become a Nazarite.
   d. in sadness that Elizabeth was barren.
3. Decide whether each statement is TRUE or FALSE. Give a verse to prove a TRUE statement; correct the FALSE statement.
   a. Mary is Deity. _____
   b. Joseph rejected the pregnant Mary. _____
   c. Mary is the Mother of God. _____
   d. Joseph was visited by an angel of the Lord. _____
   e. The word "virgin" literally means "young maiden." _____
4. Why did Mary and Joseph leave Nazareth before Jesus was born? _____
   _____
   _____
5. What sign was given the shepherds that they might recognize the new-born Savior? _____
   _____
6. Explain how decisions made by those in power in the Roman government impacted the lives of Mary and Joseph, and fulfilled prophesy surround Christ's birth. _____
   _____
   _____

Notes

3 The Naming of Jesus and the Presentation in the Temple

(Luke 2:21-38)

In keeping with the requirements of the Law of Moses, Jesus was circumcised on the eighth day. It was customary for the child to receive his name at the time of the circumcision, and Jesus received His name as the angel had instructed Joseph.

Leviticus 12, as well as Exodus 13:2, help us to understand what took place after several days. After the period of purification prescribed by the law (40 days for a male child, 80 days for a female), and in accordance with the dedication of the firstborn to the Lord, Mary fulfilled the rules of ceremonial law and brought the Child to the temple for presentation. Being of lowly circumstances, Mary and Joseph did not offer a lamb and a pigeon but a pair of turtledoves or young pigeons. One was for a burnt offering and the other for a sin offering.

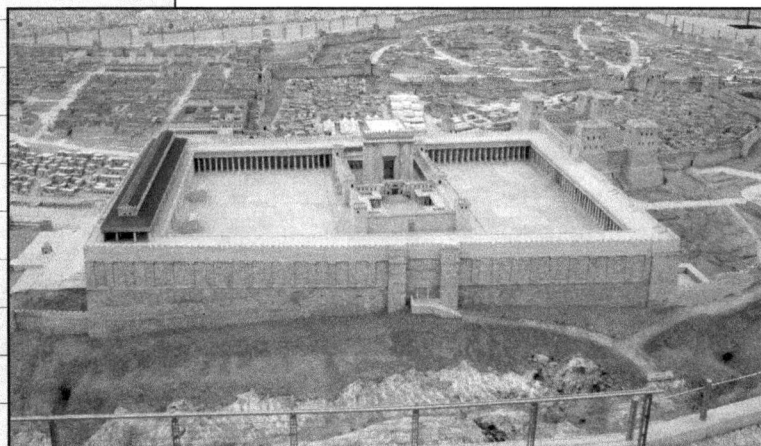

The Temple in Jerusalem at the time of Christ, as reconstructed at the Model City of Jerusalem on display at the Israel Museum.

In Jerusalem there lived a man named Simeon. He is described as "righteous and devout, looking for the consolation of Israel; and the Holy Spirit was upon him." It had been revealed to Simeon that he would not die until he had seen the Lord's Christ. Indeed, it was the Holy Spirit who led Simeon to the temple at that exact time. Seeing Jesus, Simeon took Him in his arms, praised God and acknowledged that the promise made to him had been fulfilled. He could now die for he had seen "the Lord's Christ." As we look particularly at verse 31, we see the inclusion of the Gentiles.

Men like Isaiah, who lived several centuries before the nativity, with their glorious far-reaching prophecies, such as Isaiah 52:10, were far in advance of the narrow, selfish Jewish schools of the age of Jesus Christ. It was, perhaps, the hardest lesson the apostles and first teachers of the faith had to master – this full, free admission of the vast Gentile world into the kingdom of their God. Simeon, in his song, however, distinctly repeats the broad, generous sayings of the older prophets. (*The Pulpit Commentary*, XVI: 40-41)

What did Simeon mean when he said, "Behold, this child is appointed for the fall and rise of many in Israel, and for a sign to be opposed?" While aware that others take a different view, I believe it simply means that with the coming of Jesus, many, by their reaction to Him, would be saved. Others, by their reaction to Him, would be lost. Most assuredly Jesus was a "sign to be opposed." This brings to mind Isaiah 53:3. Think of the anguish Mary would feel as the public ministry of her Son came to a close. Think of the pain Mary would experience as she stood and watched Him hang on the cross. Yet, through that very act, the true character of so many would be revealed as their hatred for righteousness and holiness culminated in the death of the Lord.

There was yet another person in the temple who would acknowledge the position of the child. It was Anna, described as a prophetess and of the tribe of Asher, a woman of great age. The tribe of Asher was one of the ten northern tribes that, through exile and intermarriage at the time of the Assyrian captivity, had all but disappeared. Some individuals, such as Anna, were able to trace their genealogy back to that tribe. Anna remained in the temple. It is apparent that by inspiration Anna knew who Jesus was and she spoke to all who would listen of what she knew.

The Magi (Matt. 2:1-12)

It appears evident that the visit of the magi took place after the presentation of the Lord in the temple. When they left, Joseph was told to take the Child and His mother to Egypt. The idea of the magi coming to Jesus on January 6 in what is called the Epiphany is completely without biblical foundation. Jesus was born in the days of Herod the king. Only Herod the Great and Herod Agrippa II held the legal title of "king." Herod Agrippa II reigned from A.D. 48 to 100, thus eliminating him from consideration.

Magi came from the east to Jerusalem. The "magi" were learned men of eastern nations, primarily from Persia and Arabia. They were devoted to the study of astronomy, religion, and medicine. The magi made the purpose of their journey clear in Jerusalem. They had come searching for the newly born king of the Jews. They had seen His star and had come to pay homage to Him. It is apparent that at this time there was a prevalent expectation in the east that some remarkable personage was to appear in Judea. There were Jews living in all parts of the known world and as they spread, they took their expectations of a Messiah with them. Two Roman historians, Seutonius and Tacitus, mention that expectation.

Herod's reaction to the visit of the magi and their purpose is not surprising. He had already executed several of his relatives that he viewed as possible threats to his throne. This news agitated Herod as yet another possible usurper to his throne was born, so he gathered together the chief priests and scribes to inquire where they looked for the Christ to be born. The answer was Bethlehem of Judea, based upon Micah 5:2. The next step Herod took to eliminate

> ## Three Things Stand Out:
> - **Jesus was born in Bethlehem of Judea.**
> - **It was in the days of Herod the king.**
> - **Magi came from the east.**

this perceived threat was to summon the magi privately and ask about the time of the appearance of the star. He was trying to determine the age of the Child. He sent the magi to Bethlehem, asking them to return to him after finding the Child, that he might come and worship Him as well.

The star guided the magi to the exact location of Jesus. When they entered into the place where Jesus and His parents were staying, they fell down and offered homage to Him, along with gifts of gold, frankincense, and myrrh. Frankincense was a fragrant gum of a tree obtained by cutting the bark. Myrrh also came from trees and was used chiefly in the embalming of the dead. To foil the murderous plans of Herod, the magi were warned in a dream not to return to him. They departed to their country by another route.

In 2007, Ehud Netzer located the tomb of Herod the Great at Herodium.

The Flight into Egypt and the Return (Matt. 2:13-23; Luke 2:39)

After the departure of the magi, the angel of the Lord appeared to Joseph with a warning to take Jesus and Mary and go to Egypt. He was to remain there until the angel appeared to him again. All of this was necessary to fulfill Hosea 11:1 and Jeremiah 31:15. When Herod saw that the magi did not return as he had expected, he issued orders that all the male children two years old and under in Bethlehem and its surrounding regions were to be executed. While this event's application to Jeremiah 31:15 is somewhat difficult to understand, and the prophecy refers initially to Rachel figuratively raising her head from her burial tomb and weeping as she saw her "sons" being carried away into Babylonian captivity, it was primarily fulfilled when Herod had the children slaughtered in Bethlehem and the areas nearby.

Archaeological date indicates that Herod the Great died in March of 4 B.C. and was succeeded by his son, Archelaus. When Herod died, an angel of the Lord appeared once again to Joseph in a dream, this time in Egypt. He instructed Joseph to take Jesus and Mary back to the land of Israel, for the one responsible for endangering the life of Jesus was dead. Joseph did as he was told and it appears that he intended to return to Judea, perhaps to Bethlehem, but changed his mind when he found out that Archelaus reigned in his father's stead in Judea. He received an additional warning from God in a dream and went to Galilee instead, specifically to Nazareth. This was also in fulfillment of prophecy, "He shall be called a Nazarene." There is no statement found in the Old Testament worded in that way. However, it most likely means that Jesus would be of a humble life and would be despised and rejected as prophesied by several of the prophets. That certainly occurred, as Galilee was a region of less than stellar reputation and Nazareth apparently looked down upon as well. Nathanael would later say to Philip, "Can any good thing come out of Nazareth?" (John 1:46). Luke did not write of the visit of the magi, the flight into Egypt, and the slaughter of the children but went directly from the presentation in the temple to their settling in Nazareth.

Questions

1. How did Jesus get His name? _____
   _____

2. How do you explain that Simeon and the prophetess Anna knew that Jesus was the Christ when they had never seen Him?_____
   _____

3. How did Herod try using the magi to his own advantage and how were his plans thwarted? _____
   _____

4. Why did Mary and Joseph go to Egypt? _____
   _____

5. Under what circumstances did they finally journey to Nazareth?_____
   _____

6. What statements below about the magi are TRUE?
   a. They arrived at the manger in Bethlehem to honor the newly born Christ._____
   b. They were from the region around Judea._____
   c. They found the Christ child by accident. _____
   d. They were educated men from the East. _____
   e. We can know for sure that there were three magi because they carried three gifts. _____
   f. They were sent to Bethlehem by Herod. _____
   g. They returned to Herod with news of the child. _____

4 The Childhood of Jesus

(Luke 2:40-52)

After the return from Egypt and settlement in Nazareth, all we know of the first twelve years of the Lord's life is that He developed as other children develop. He grew and became strong and increased in wisdom. We do know that Jesus did not sin and that He was God in the flesh. The passage also tells us that "the grace of God was upon Him." In normal New Testament usage, grace means unmerited favor. Here it simply means favor. Jesus was well pleasing in the sight of God and blessed by Him. To state any more about His development and childhood would be pure speculation.

The Wailing Wall, is a retaining wall for the Herodian Temple (see p. 12); today it is the site for the Bar and Bath Mitzveh of young Jewish children.

Every year the parents of Jesus went to Jerusalem for the Passover. This was one of three feasts a year in observance of which Jewish males were to present themselves before the Lord. This requirement is found in Exodus 23:14-17. The Jewish custom would come to be for those within a 20 mile radius of the city of Jerusalem.

When Jesus was twelve years old, He accompanied His parents to the Passover feast in Jerusalem. After they had fulfilled the days, which would have been a total of eight – one day for the killing of the Paschal lamb and seven days in observance of the feast of unleavened bread – they began their journey home. Mary and Joseph believed Jesus to be with them. In fact, He had tarried in Jerusalem. Ultimately Mary and Joseph discovered that Jesus was not with them, and after searching among the company with whom they

Differences Between Baptism of John and of Jesus	
John's Baptism	**Jesus' Baptism**
John's baptism temporary	Baptism of Jesus final – the one baptism of Eph. 4
John's baptism preparatory	Baptism in name of Jesus is into Christ
At time of John's baptism Jesus had not died	Baptism of Jesus into His death

were traveling, returned to Jerusalem to search for Him. After three days they found Him, sitting in the temple among the rabbis, listening to them and asking them questions. According to the Talmud, in the temple enclosure there were three synagogues – one at the gate of the court of the Gentiles, one in the southeast part of the inner court, and one at the entrance to the court of the Israelites. It was in these structures that the doctors of the law, the rabbis, would sit and expound upon the law.

Everyone who heard Jesus was amazed at the depth of understanding He displayed concerning the law and at the intelligence of His answers. There was a slight reproach in Mary's words, "Son, why have you treated us this way? Behold, your father and I have been anxiously looking for you?" The answer of Jesus is profound: "Why is it that you were looking for me? Did you not know that I had to be about my Father's business?" Certainly Mary remembered the circumstances of His birth and who His father truly was. However, now the veil of silence descends again as Jesus returns to Nazareth, there to subject Himself as an obedient child. But Mary kept these things in her heart.

John Begins His Work (Matt. 3:1-6; Mark 1:1-6; Luke 3:1-6)

Tiberius was the emperor of Rome. Pontius Pilate was the governor of Judea. Herod Antipas was the tetrarch of Galilee (tetrarch–ruler of a fourth part). His brother Philip was tetrarch of Ituraea and Trachonitis, and Lysanias was tetrarch of Abilene. Annas and Caiaphas were the high priests. Annas was the rightful high priest, but he had been deposed by the Roman procurator, Gratus, in A.D. 14. Caiaphas was his son-in-law and had been appointed in his place. Note how carefully Luke set the time.

"In those days" John came into the wilderness of Judea, clothed in a coat of camel's hair and a plain leather girdle, eating the wild locusts and honey. He preached a "baptism of repentance for the forgiveness of sins," because the kingdom of heaven was at hand. I believe that a person sincerely baptized with John's baptism had his sins forgiven in the same way a devout Jew had his sins forgiven on the Day of Atonement. Confronted by the full gospel of our Lord Jesus, a person would have to respond and be baptized into the death of Christ for the remission of sins (Acts 19:1-5). John's work was in fulfillment of prophecy. Isaiah 40:3-5 is quoted, and Mark quotes Malachi 3:1.

The Preaching of John the Baptist (Matt. 3:7-12; Mark 1:7-8; Luke 3:7-18)

The preaching done by John disturbed the religious leaders of the Jews and stirred the hearts of the common people. Matthew specifically mentions the Pharisees and Sadducees being the recipients of a scathing rebuke. Luke indi-

Notes

cates the entire multitude was included. The rebuke was, "You brood of vipers, who warned you to flee from the wrath to come?" The viper was an extremely poisonous serpent, two to five feet in length and about an inch in diameter. It symbolized guile and malice, cunning and venom. What a way to be described, and it calls into question their motivation for coming to hear him. But regardless of their motivation, John made it clear that he was demanding change. They had to repent. The fact that they were Jews, physical descendants of Abraham, did not guarantee their citizenship in the kingdom of the Messiah, although that is what they thought. However, mere preaching without practical application accomplishes little. As the multitude came to him asking the question, "Then what shall we do?" John gave them simple, practical applications. Be unselfish, be generous. Demonstrate repentance. A publican came; soldiers came.

To people of a heightened Messianic expectation, it was only natural that some would begin to speculate as to whether or not he might be the Christ. John moved to lay to rest to such thinking. Yes, he did baptize them in water unto repentance. But there was One coming who was inherently superior to John, One whose shoes John was not worthy to loosen. John was His forerunner. The One who was coming would baptize with "the Holy Spirit and with fire." I am of the conviction that the "baptism with the Holy Spirit" refers to what took place in Acts 2 when the Apostles were completely immersed in the Holy Spirit. It occurred again in Acts 10 with Cornelius and his household. The "baptism with fire," contextually, must refer to eternal punishment. It corresponds to the unfruitful trees being cast into the fire and the chaff being burned up. Also, John used another illustration. In those days, wheat and other grains were harvested by hand. Being picked, the grain was beaten or trodden on by oxen on a smooth, hard piece of ground call the threshing-floor. It was picked up in a winnowing fan and tossed into the air. The wind blew the chaff away and the clean grain fell back to the floor. The grain was kept, and the chaff was burned. The One who was coming would separate the good from the wicked.

Jesus Is Baptized (Matt. 3:13-17; Mark 1:9-11; Luke 3:21-22)

Jesus left Nazareth to journey to the region around Jordan where John was baptizing. Jesus came "to be baptized by him," at John's hands, thus linking John's work to His. As Jesus came to be baptized, John sought to prevent Him from doing so, saying, "I have need to be baptized by you, and you come to me." In His response Jesus intimated that John was correct. He did not need the baptism of repentance for remission of sins for He was sinless. Nevertheless, to "fulfill all righteousness," carrying out the decrees of the Father, He would be baptized. After His baptism, Luke tells us that Jesus was praying and the heaven was opened, and the Holy Spirit descended upon Him in bodily form like a dove. Accompanying this was a voice from heaven saying, "Thou art My beloved Son, in Thee I am well-pleased."

The descent of the Holy Spirit upon Jesus was in fulfillment of a prophecy found in Isaiah 11:2. When the Holy Spirit descended upon Jesus, and John would later testify, "I have beheld the Spirit descending as a dove out of heaven, and He remained upon him" (John 1:32), He received the promised anointing of the Spirit. What of the multitude? Did they hear the voice and see the dove? I do not believe that they saw and understood for such would have been a very early announcement of Jesus as the Messiah, and the Lord would often say on later occasions that His time had not yet come. John and Jesus saw, heard, and understood.

Questions

1. What do we know of Jesus' childhood? _____
_____

2. Does Jesus reflect characteristics of Deity or humanity from His early years?
_____
_____

3. Why did Luke feel it was important to include the political structure that existed as John began his preaching? _____
_____

4. How was it obvious that people did not understand the nature of John's message? _____
_____

5. Why would John's message disturb the Jewish leaders? _____
_____

6. Under what circumstances does John use the following images:
   a. "brood of vipers" _____
   b. the wheat and the chaff _____
   c. "baptism with fire"_____

7. What was the difference between the baptism that John taught and the baptism of the gospel of Jesus Christ? _____
_____

8. Why did John first reject the notion of baptizing Jesus? _____
_____

9. Why did Jesus insist on being baptized? _____
_____

10. Were those baptized by John subject to baptism once they accepted the gospel of Jesus Christ? Why or why not? _____
_____

Notes

5

The Temptation

(Matt. 4:1-11; Mark 1:12-13; Luke 4:1-13)

Jesus was tempted for forty days and nights in the Wilderness of Judea.

We should address the reality of what our Lord faced. The temptations were real. Having taken upon Himself humanity, He felt the temptations as we do. Hebrews 4:15 tells us, "For we do not have a high priest who cannot sympathize with our weaknesses, but One who has been tempted in all things as we are, yet without sin." Those who argue that Jesus was God and did not feel the temptations the way we do miss the point entirely. No one knows temptation to the extent that Jesus did. At some point all of us give in and succumb to it. Jesus reached that point and went beyond, never failing. Do we want to know how to endure temptation? Look to the One who experienced it at its zenith and never gave in.

By combining Matthew and Luke's accounts, we know that immediately following His baptism, Jesus was led by the Spirit into the wilderness to be tempted by the devil. There He fasted for 40 days and 40 nights. Was Jesus tempted throughout the 40 days or did the temptations not come until after the fast had ended? Matthew certainly makes it appear that the temptations occurred after the fast; Mark and Luke make it appear continuous. I believe that during the 40 days temptations of various kinds were presented to Jesus, with the three specifically mentioned coming after the fast and being representative of them all.

The first recorded temptation – "If you are the Son of God, command that these stones become bread." This brings to mind the "lust of the flesh" John wrote of in 1 John 2:16. Jesus was hungry. Would He use His miraculous power in a selfish way? He quoted Deuteronomy 8:3. He resorted to God's word, the source of all answers. The most important is not physical in nature. It is spiritual.

The second temptation (according to Matthew – Luke places it third) – Jesus was taken to a high pinnacle of the temple and told, "If you are the Son of God throw yourself down; for it is written, He will give His angels charge over you; and on their hands they will bear you up, lest you strike your foot against a stone." This calls to mind John's words of 1 John 2:16, "the pride of life." The temptation, through the misuse of Scripture, was to tempt Jesus to endanger His life for no other purpose than to prove protection of and close communion with His Father. Jesus responded with Deuteronomy 6:16.

The third temptation (second in Luke) – The devil took Jesus to an exceeding high mountain, showing Him all the kingdoms of the world and the glory of them. This happened in a "moment of time," showing the supernatural nature of what was taking place. If Jesus was to worship Satan, He would give the Lord all that could be seen. This brings to mind "the lust of the eyes" (1 John 2:16).

Jesus once again answered with Scripture, this time Deuteronomy 6:13. This terrible period of trial and testing at an end, the angels came and ministered unto Jesus.

John Identifies Jesus as Christ (John 1:19-34)

John made it very clear to those who had been sent by the Jewish leaders that he was not the Christ. He was not the prophet Elijah come again – although Malachi 4:5 makes it clear that one would come in the spirit of Elijah, and Jesus would clearly identify John as the fulfillment of that prophecy in Matthew 11:14. John made it clear that he was not the Prophet, a reference to Deuteronomy 18:15. He was the fulfillment of Isaiah 40:3; he was the voice of one crying in the wilderness, making straight the way of the Lord.

Those who were representing the Pharisees asked why John was baptizing if he was none of those mentioned? By baptizing he was making followers of himself; but John made it clear that he was simply preparing the way for One who was coming, One much greater than himself.

After the questioning by the delegation sent from the Jewish leaders, the following day John saw Jesus coming and declared, "Behold, the Lamb of God who takes away the sin of the world!" By referring to Jesus as "the Lamb," John immediately introduced to his Jewish hearers the idea of sacrifice. Lambs were commonly used for sin-offerings (Lev. 4:32). A lamb was killed for the celebration of Passover. By referring to Jesus as "the Lamb of *God,*" John identified Him as the lamb or sacrifice that God provided and as the only true and perfect offering for sin. Hebrews 10:4-10 should be read in connection to John's pronouncement. By saying that Jesus was "the Lamb of God *who takes away the sin of the world,*" John was speaking of the vicarious nature of the sacrifice of the Lord. Did all understand what he meant?

John continued by clearly stating that Jesus was the One about whom he had spoken. Even though Jesus was born after John, John rightly stated, "For He existed before me." This was true in the sense of primacy and in the absolute sense as we have already seen that Jesus is eternal. John went into further detail about the baptism of the Lord. John knew what his mission was. He was to prepare the way for the Lord. God had given John his mission and had given him the way to identify the Messiah: "He upon whom you see the Spirit descending and remaining upon Him, this is the one who baptizes in the Holy Spirit." John saw the Spirit descend and declared Jesus to be the Son of God.

The First Disciples (John 1:35-51)

On the next day two of John's disciples were standing with the Baptist and heard him testify of Jesus. I believe that one of these disciples was John, the author of this gospel. From this time forward he writes as an eyewitness; there is no other account in the gospel of his call to discipleship. Several other times in the gospel John withholds his name. These two heard and followed. When Jesus saw them following, He asked, "What do ye seek?" When they answered, "Where are you staying?" we find the challenge of Christianity – "Come and see." It was four in the afternoon according to the Jewish method of keeping time. Andrew, before doing anything else, gives us our first example of the passionate evangelistic fervor that should characterize all disciples of Jesus: "He first found his own brother, Simon, and said to him, We have found the Messiah." Peter came and the Lord saw in Peter what he could be, tracing the course of his future with the words, "You are Simon the son of John, you shall be called Cephas." Cephas means "stone."

Notes

The next day Jesus began to make His way to Galilee. He came across Philip and said simply, "Follow me." Just as Andrew had gone to share the good news, so did Philip. He found Nathanael and called Jesus, "Him of whom Moses in the Law and also the Prophets wrote." To Nathanael's skepticism, Philip simply said, "Come and see." Nathanael's reaction is interesting. He did not immediately burst forth with rejoicing. He was a Galilean (John 21:2), and well aware of the reputation of Nazareth. Galilee in general lacked the culture of Judah, had a crude dialect of speech, and a large population of Gentiles. When Nathanael did come and Jesus identified him as "an Israelite indeed, in whom is no guile," Nathanael was surprised. How did this man know who he was? Yet even before Philip had called him, Jesus had known who he was. The Lord had not just seen Nathanael under a fig tree in a natural way – it was supernatural. That truth is seen in the faith that it caused in Nathanael. He regarded the revelation of his character and whereabouts as a great thing; yet Jesus assured him that he was destined to see far greater things.

Questions

1. Decide whether each of the following is TRUE or FALSE. Prove the TRUE statement with a verse of Scripture. Make the FALSE statement TRUE.
   a. Temptation is sin. _____
   b. The account of the temptation of Christ was a parable. _____
   _____
   c. Satan came to produce sin in Christ. _____
   d. Satan was convinced of Christ's divinity. _____
   e. God led Jesus into temptation. _____
   f. Christ could not be tempted as we are. _____

2. Show how the appeal of each temptation was consistent with John's description of sin in 1 John 2:16._____
   _____

3. Tell why Jesus responds to each temptation with the following Scripture:
   a. Deuteronomy 8:3 _____
   b. Deuteronomy 6:16 _____
   c. Deuteronomy 6:13 _____

4. What was John the Baptist's purpose? _____
   _____

5. Explain the significance of the reference to Jesus as "the lamb of God who takes away sin of the world." _____
   _____

6. Explain how Christ is our Passover._____
   _____

7. How did the Spirit descend on Jesus? _____
   _____

8. How did Peter, Andrew, John, Philip, and Nathaniel become the first disciples of Jesus? _____
   _____

9. How are Christians "chosen" today? _____
   _____

10. "We have found the Messiah." Explain the significance of Andrew's statement.
   _____

6

The First Miracle

(John 2:1-11)

The miracle took place in Cana of Galilee, apparently a small village located about three hours' journey northeast of Nazareth. The first miracle occurred not in the city of Jerusalem where it could have been witnessed by a greater number of people and certainly would have received greater notoriety. It took place in the relative privacy of a wedding feast in a small, rather insignificant village. It happened at a wedding feast. Jesus clearly held marriage as honorable and did not teach that celibacy is inherently superior. In addition, a wedding feast was an occasion of joy and happiness in which Jesus readily participated. He was not a withdrawn ascetic. Jesus took part in the innocent joys of life. Being a follower of Christ does not mean a life of constant denial of anything of a physical nature that brings happiness. Being a follower of Christ enables us to enjoy to the fullest the pure and innocent things of this life.

There are several villages laying claim to being Cana, where Jesus' first miracle was performed. These stone pots are displayed at the Franciscan Church in Khirbet Cana.

It is important to consider what prompted the miracle. The wine was gone. The supply had proven to be inadequate for whatever reason, and those responsible for the feast would have had to face the embarrassment of not having sufficient refreshments for their guests. In His actions we can see the kindness of the Lord. Jesus taught us to relieve suffering, elevate the lowly, and show concern for all people, even those of the most humble circumstances. Jesus helped them. Mary simply told him, "They have no wine." It does not appear to me that Mary knew what Jesus would do, simply that He could do something. She was aware of the unique nature of her son. To what extent we can only guess. Our study of Luke 2:51 surely indicates that she thought deeply about Jesus, about His relationship to His Father, and the work He was come to do. The Lord's reply, "Woman, what do I have to do with you? My hour has not yet come," is both a statement of respect and gentle rebuke. Two things are apparent from His answer. One, the time of His subjection to Mary and Joseph (if he was still alive) was over. His work as the Messiah had begun. Secondly, the time to *reveal* His full work had not yet come. It was not time to reveal His messianic claims. It was not time to make Who He was known to the general populace. Mary told the servants, "Whatever He says to you, do it."

Six stone waterpots, containing altogether 120 gallons to as much as 180 gallons, were filled to the brim with water at the word of Jesus. That which had

Monies from all countries were converted into the Tryian Shekel to be used in paying Temple taxes.

John 2:20 says, "It has taken forty-six years to build this temple, and will You raise it up in three days?" This is an important text for dating the ministry of Jesus. Herod the Great began rebuilding the Temple in 20 B.C. Since then, 46 years had elapsed, making the time of the events in John 2 about A.D. 26-27.

been water was now wine. Without a recorded word from Jesus, the water was changed. It was done immediately. There were no delays, no long incantations, no anxious moments over whether the miracle would take place or not. It was done perfectly. The headwaiter pronounced the wine to be good, better than the wine originally served. This was the beginning of many signs that Jesus would perform; signs that would show forth His glory and lead many to faith.

Capernaum (John 2:12)

After working His first miracle; Jesus, His mother, His brothers, and His disciples went to Capernaum and stayed for a few days. Capernaum was located on the northwest shore of the Sea of Galilee, about two and one half miles southwest of the point where the headwaters of the River Jordan enter the sea. Capernaum will be discussed, along with Jesus locating there, in future lessons.

The First Cleansing of the Temple (John 2:13-25)

The first cleansing of the temple took place at the Passover Feast, the first of four such feasts that Jesus would observe during His public ministry. It was one of the three great annual feasts of the Jews. The others were Pentecost and the Feast of Tabernacles. Vast crowds would flock to the city of Jerusalem and the temple would be the focal point of activity. The streets would have been thronged with the multitudes moving toward the temple and the temple itself further crowded by the merchants selling sheep, oxen, and doves. There were also the tables of the money changers. Money changers were necessary because of a law established in Exodus 30:11-16. Twenty days before the Passover, the priests began to collect this half shekel paid yearly by every adult Israelite, rich or poor, as atonement money for his soul and to be applied to the expenses of the temple. Different kinds of money were in circulation from many different countries, with some of it defiled by heathen symbols and inscriptions. It was not lawful to pay with this kind of money. Therefore, an individual would go to the money changers to receive the proper coin in exchange for such currency and generally be charged five percent interest on the exchange. This merchandising would have been excusable as necessary, if it had been confined to the streets leading to the temple. However, the considerable space of the Court of the Gentiles within the temple precinct were used by the merchants and money changers as their marketplace.

Filled with righteous indignation at this abuse of His Father's house, Jesus fashioned a whip of several small cords and unleashed His divine wrath upon those who so abused the temple. He drove out the sheep and the oxen and those who tended them. He turned over the tables of the money changers, spilling their coins onto the floor of the Court of the Gentiles. He told those selling doves, "Take these things away; stop making my Father's house a house of merchandise." Seeing His righteous indignation, His disciples remembered Psalm 69:9. It is interesting that the leaders of the Jews did not dare to condemn Jesus for what He had done. Instead, they asked for some sign that would indicate that He had the right or authority to act as He had. Jesus responded with, "Destroy this temple, and in three days I will raise it up." They had no idea that Jesus was speaking of His crucifixion and resurrection – two events that this day certainly helped to set in motion. Later, after the Lord had risen from the dead, His disciples would remember these words and have their faith strengthened.

While still in Jerusalem for the Passover Feast, Jesus performed many miracles witnessed by a number of people. This caused many to believe in Him, but Jesus, knowing all men, would not entrust Himself to them. He knew their thoughts, character, and the meaning of and reason for their faith.

Conversation With Nicodemus (John 3:1-22)

Nicodemus was a Pharisee, a ruler of the Jews and willing to investigate, yet he came by night. Perhaps as an earnest seeker of truth he desired the in-depth, private conversation that, due to the crowds, could not be had during the day. It is also possible that this shows a certain timidity in Nicodemus. He wanted to know of Jesus, but not in full view of the public. Later we will find Nicodemus seeking to check the injustice and rash actions of his fellow leaders, but his objection will be based upon a general principle and betrayed none of his personal beliefs concerning Jesus. Later still we find him stepping forth to bury Jesus after someone else, Joseph of Arimathea, apparently took the initiative.

It appears that Nicodemus had two things on his mind; one he would state, the other Jesus simply understood. Bear in mind that Nicodemus was a scholar. His first remarks to Jesus indicate his philosophic turn of mind. He had weighed the evidence and had reached a logical conclusion, yet his great learning also presented some problems. Nicodemus' conclusion fell so far short of the truth that Jesus moved directly to what must have been on the scholar's mind in the first place. Here was Nicodemus' opportunity to speak to One who the evidence indicated was sent from God. Sweeping aside the conclusion Nicodemus had reached, Jesus went right to the heart of the matter. "Truly, truly, I say unto you, unless one is born again, he cannot see the kingdom of God." Failing to grasp the spiritual significance of what Jesus had said, Nicodemus approached it from a purely physical standpoint: "How can a man be born when he is old? He cannot enter a second time into his mother's womb and be born, can he?" The response, "Truly, truly, I say to you, unless one is born of water and the Spirit, he cannot enter into the kingdom of God." This is one action, the redemption of one individual soul. The birth of water refers to baptism; the birth of Spirit seems to suggest the whole spiritual transformation that occurs when the Holy Spirit comes into contact with the spirit of man through the preaching of the Word and man comes from the world into the glorious kingdom of God. Taken together, this describes the new birth. The physical birth and the spiritual birth to which Jesus referred are two separate and distinct things.

"How can these things be?" The possibility of God bringing a man forth into a new, spiritual kingdom should not have astonished Nicodemus any more than the very forces of nature which are controlled by God but surpass human understanding. Jesus asked him, "Are you the teacher of Israel, and do not understand these things?" Jesus spoke of things about which he had personal knowledge. If Nicodemus could not understand the earthly things, how could he understand the heavenly?

In His continued conversation with Nicodemus, Jesus spoke of the coming salvation of man, made possible through the sufferings and exaltation of the Son. His reference to the serpent being lifted up calls to mind Numbers 21. There Moses constructed a serpent of brass, per God's instructions, and lifted it up. Those who looked upon it were saved from the bites of the serpents in the camp. Those who did not look upon it perished. In much the same way Jesus would be lifted up and those who came to Him in obedient faith would be saved. The Lord spoke of the love of God, manifested in the sending of His only begotten Son, not to judge, but to save. He spoke of the deliverance of those

Notes

who have faith in Him and are faithful to Him. He also spoke of the condemnation that would fall on those who willfully rejected the truth.

After His conversation with Nicodemus, Jesus left Jerusalem and went into the country of Judea with His disciples. While there the Lord taught, and many were baptized. John 4:2 indicates that the Lord's disciples baptized, not Jesus Himself.

Questions

1. What was Jesus' motive in supplying the wine at the wedding feast? _____
   a. To show His power to the guests in attendance
   b. To relieve the concerns and anxiety of the host
   c. To show Himself as the Messiah
   d. To act at the request of the host

2. What did Jesus mean when He said, "My hour has not yet come"?_____
   _____

3. Why was *filling the pot to the brim with water* significant to answering the skeptics that this account was a miracle? _____
   _____

4. What was the result of Jesus' first miracle? _____
   _____

5. Was Jesus the only child of Mary and His earthly father Joseph? Explain your answer. _____
   _____

6. After reading Exodus 30:11-16 explain why the money changers were necessary._____
   _____

7. What made the merchandising experience Jesus encountered unacceptable to Him? _____
   _____

8. How did Jesus view the behavior as an abuse of His Father's house?_____
   _____

9. When asked why He had the authority to disrupt the merchants, Jesus replied, "Destroy the temple and I will raise it up." In particular He was speaking of_____.

10. What brought Nicodemus to Christ? _____
    _____

11. Nicodemus confused the _____ with the _____ .

12. How is "one born of the water"? _____
    _____

13. What does "one born of the Spirit" refer to? _____
    _____

14. Read John 3:16 and explain how the verse is really a summary of the message of the gospel._____
    _____

15. Explain how God's judgment is not arbitrary._____
    _____
    _____

7

John Continues His Work

(John 3:23-36)

John continued his work as long as he had opportunities. John was teaching and baptizing in Aenon near Salim because there was much water there. People were still coming to hear John, still coming to be baptized by him. While there, a dispute arose between John's disciples and some of the Jews concerning purification (or religious washing). In conjunction with this, some of John's disciples came to him with a complaint about Jesus. Jesus' baptism was detracting from John's. After all, John had borne witness to Jesus and it was as if Jesus was doing something that John had originated. More people were coming to Jesus than to John.

John's Answer
- **Acknowledged Jesus' divine authority**
- **Reminded his disciples of his testimony concerning Jesus**
- **Spoke of the great satisfaction he had in the advance of the Lord's work**
- **Spoke clearly of the need for Jesus to increase and John to decrease**
- **Acknowledged the superiority of Jesus, even spoke of His divine origin**
- **Spoke of the teaching of Jesus, its divine origin and veracity**

Jesus in Samaria (John 4:1-42)

The growth of Jesus' ministry was coming to the attention of the Pharisees. It may be that the animosity they felt toward Jesus, the animosity that would continue to grow and reach its climax in the death on Calvary, was beginning to be expressed. Jesus determined that it was time to move on, and He left Judea to depart for Galilee. Normally the Jews would take a route that enabled them to bypass Samaria, but not Jesus. He chose to go through Samaria and for a few glorious days, the Samaritans would hear Jesus.

The journey was arduous and by the sixth hour, noon according to the Jewish method of accounting time, Jesus and His disciples had reached the city of Sychar, near the site of Jacob's well. Jesus, fully God and fully man, was weary and sat on the well to rest. While there, a Samaritan woman came to draw water. Jesus, His disciples having left to purchase food, requested a drink of water from the woman. Her reply makes two interesting points. Jesus was a Jew and she was a Samaritan. The passage itself tells us, "For Jews have no dealings with Samaritans." She was also a woman. Jewish social customs of the time precluded speaking to a woman on the street.

Who were the Samaritans? They were a hybrid race of people resulting from the intermarriage of the remnant of the ten tribes of Israel left in Israel with the colonies of heathen nations brought in when Samaria fell in 722-721 B.C. The Assyrians took the best of Israel into captivity and deported the intellectual and political elite of the nation. Only the feebler elements of the nation were left in Israel, and as they intermarried with the heathen brought in by Assyria, they eventually lost their Jewish identity. We can find bitter hostility existing between the Jews and Samaritans as early as the reconstruction of Jerusalem during the time of Ezra and Nehemiah.

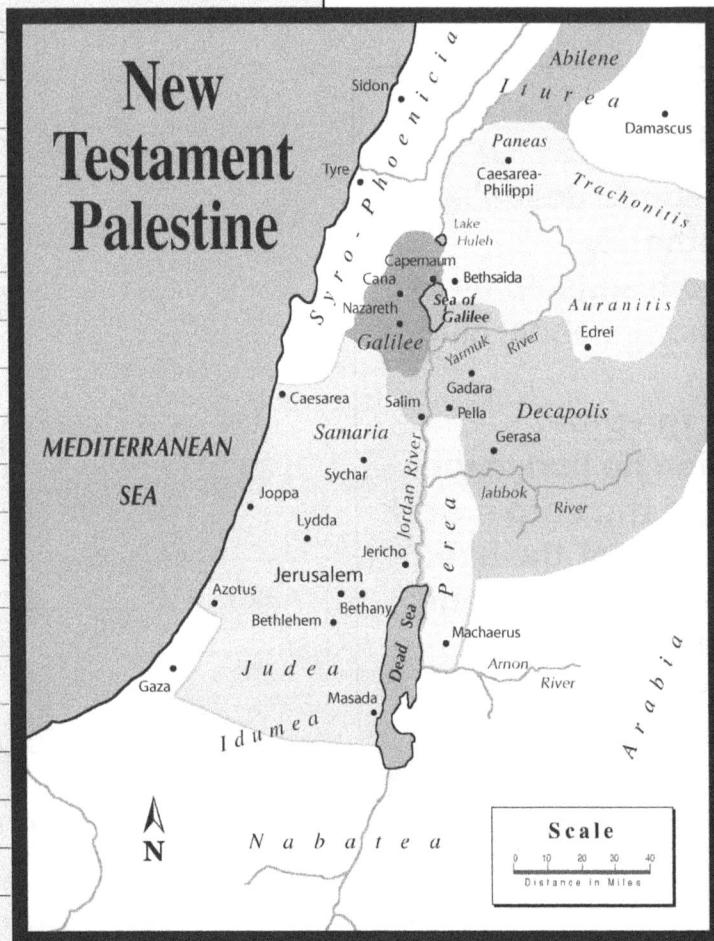

New Testament Palestine

In His reply to the woman, Jesus turned the discussion to the subject of God. You may recall that in the exchange with Nicodemus Jesus had introduced the subject of the new birth. Here he speaks of the "gift of God" and of the "living water." Just like Nicodemus, the Samaritan woman took Jesus' words in a purely physical sense. Jesus continued in the spiritual. Those who drank the water of Jacob's well would thirst again. However, those who drank of the living water would never thirst. They would have "a well of water springing up to eternal life." The woman wanted some of this water so that she would never be thirsty and never have to draw water again. Jesus said, "Go, call your husband, and come here."

This woman had a need for what Jesus had. She had had five husbands and was with a man now to whom she was not married. She had said that she had no husband and to that extent she was telling the truth. However, with reference to her checkered past, Jesus had revealed Himself a little more fully. How could He have known these things if He were not a prophet of God? The woman arrived at the same conclusion with which the learned Nicodemus had started his conversation with Jesus. The woman said, "Sir, I perceive that you are a prophet."

There appears to be two ways to look at the woman's next question. It is possible that speaking to one she perceives to be a prophet and realizing her spiritual need, she was seeking an answer to an old controversy. Being a member of an outcast race, she was unable to go to Jerusalem for worship. Her forefathers had worshipped at Mt. Gerizim. Which was the proper place for worship – Jerusalem or Mt. Gerizim? It is also possible that being confronted with her sinful past, she was simply trying to change the subject.

Whatever might have been the motivation, Jesus denied the appeal for Mt. Gerizim. The claims of the Samaritans were invalid. They had abandoned all but the first five books of the Old Testament. The Old Testament was the Word of God; salvation was of the Jews in the sense that the Messiah would come through them, and the Samaritan claims were absolutely false. However, if she was appealing for an approach to God, that was not denied. Jesus taught her that it was not a matter of location, but of spirit and truth in finding God. The heart must be involved in worship but it must be combined with the truth – God's truth - or the worship is worthless. Indeed, a new revelation was being granted from heaven that would demonstrate the fulfillment of the Old Testament and beginning of the New. All of this was contained in the Lord's answer and makes it one of the most profound and revolutionary statements found in the gospels.

In their conversation Jesus had taken it beyond the water of Jacob's well and offered "living water." He revealed miraculous insight into her ungodly past and condemned it. He had even, in a veiled way, claimed superiority to the Old Testament itself and the authority to reveal a new way from God. Then the conversation turned to the Messiah. The woman said, "I know that Messiah is coming (He who is called Christ); when the One comes, He will declare all things to us." Jesus said, "I who speak to you am He."

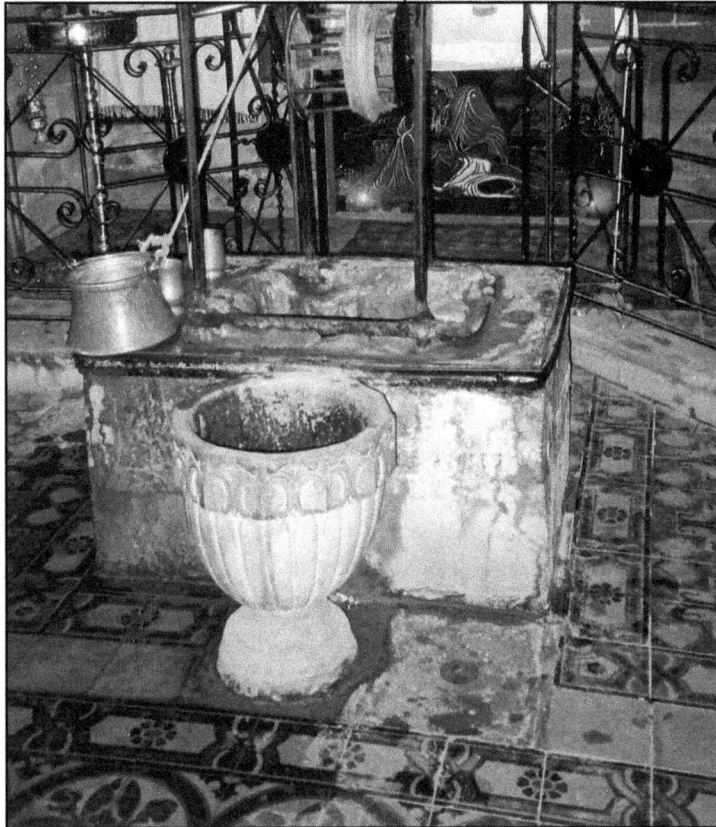
Jacob's well in modern Nablus is the location of Jesus' meeting with the Samaritan woman.

Sitting on a well in the outcast land of Samaria, talking to a woman of a sordid past, alone with her and away from all the crowds, Jesus revealed Himself as He truly is. He was, and He is, the Messiah! Just as the climax of the conversation had been reached, the disciples came back with the provisions they had purchased. They were surprised to find Jesus talking to this woman. The woman, having come to Jacob's well to draw water, left her water pot and ran into the city. Her enthusiastic announcement to the men of the city caused them to abandon all and come to see for themselves.

In the meantime Jesus taught His disciples that the truly important things in life are not the physical needs that we feel and experience. The truly important thing is doing the work of God while the harvest is ripe. For two days Jesus stayed in the midst of the Samaritans, teaching them and having their faith in Him as the Messiah grow and be confirmed.

John Arrested (Luke 3:19-20)

I have chosen to place the arrest of John the Baptist here because we know that John was present in Judea at the same time Jesus was teaching and His disciples baptizing. Also, the next time we read of John, he is sending messengers to Jesus from prison (Luke 7). Matthew and Mark both indicate that John's being "cast into prison" was one of the Lord's reasons for departing to Galilee.

Herod Antipas was the son of Herod the Great and Malthace, a Samaritan woman. Half Idumaean, half Samaritan, he had therefore not a drop of Jewish blood in his veins, and "Galilee of the Gentiles" seemed a fit dominion for such a prince. He ruled as 'tetrarch' of Galilee and Peraea from 4 B.C. to 39 A.D. The gospel picture we have of him is far from prepossessing. He is superstitious, foxlike in his cunning and wholly immoral. John the Baptist was brought into his life through an open rebuke of his gross immorality and the defiance of the laws of Moses… (ISBE, III: 1381)

Herodias was the daughter of Aristobulus, son of Herod the Great, by Mariamne, daughter of Hyrcanus. Herod Antipas was the son of Herod the Great by Malthace. Herod Antipas was thus the step-brother of Aristobulus, father of Herodias (ISBE, III: 1383)

John boldly rebuked Herod because he had taken his brother Philip's wife, Herodias, to be his own wife. Because of the rebuke, Herod had John cast into prison. Added to his list of sins was the unlawful and unwarranted imprisonment of John.

Questions

1. What were the complaints of John's disciples concerning the baptisms by Jesus? _____

2. Show how it is obvious they didn't understand the true nature of John's mission. _____

3. Why did the disciples feel uncomfortable about Jesus talking to the Samaritan woman? _____

4. Explain why Samaritans were considered **inferior** by the Jewish leaders. _____

5. What is different about the "living water" which Christ will provide and the water from Jacob's well? _____

6. What made the woman at the well think Jesus was a prophet? _____

7. What do we learn from Christ's encounter with the Samaritan woman as recorded in John 4? _____

8. Check all of the statements which are TRUE about Herod Antipas:
   a. Son of "Herod the Great" _____
   b. Jewish _____
   c. Eager to learn from the message of John _____
   d. Believed Jesus was the Messiah _____
   e. Tetrarch of Galilee and Peraea _____
   f. Wise and responsible _____
   g. Took his brother's wife _____
9. Why was John imprisoned? _____
   _____

8 The Galilean Ministry Begins

(Matt. 4:12-17; Mark 1:14-15; Luke 4:14-15; John 4:43-45)

After learning of John's arrest, Jesus left Judea for Galilee. He went through Samaria into Galilee and specifically the city of Nazareth. He left there to go to Capernaum, a city we have already discussed. Matthew pointed out the significance of Jesus making Galilee the recipient of the bulk of His ministry. It was in fulfillment of prophecy (Isa. 9:1-2). Galilee of the nations, or Galilee of the Gentiles, was the region primarily of the tribes of Zebulun and Naphtali. The area was bordered by a number of heathen nations. Not only were there many Gentiles living in the vicinity of Galilee, many lived in the region itself. This would appear to explain the less than favorable view most Jews held concerning Galilee, as evidenced by Nathanael's question in John 1. However, there was glory and honor to be had for this region. A "light" would shine among them. This occurred when Jesus fixed His residence in Capernaum.

> Christ passed the greatest part of his public ministry in Galilee; there lay Capernaum, his ordinary place of abode; in Galilee were most of his disciples; there he performed many miracles; there the preaching of the gospel met with much success. . . . Altogether similar is the passage in the first verse of the fifth chapter of Micah. . . . As there, the birth of the Messiah shall confer honor upon the hitherto obscure Bethlehem, so here shall Galilee, hitherto held in contempt, upon which the Jews cast reproach that no prophet arose there, be raised to honor and rendered illustrious by the manifestation of the Messiah (Hengstenberg, *Christology of the Old Testament,* 174).

Thus Jesus went to Galilee. It was time for Him to manifest Himself more fully. Capernaum was made His base of operations and the people of Galilee were ready to receive Him. As He went through the region teaching in the synagogues, He called upon the Jews to repent and believe His gospel, for the kingdom of heaven was at hand. As He worked, His fame spread throughout the land.

The Healing of the Royal Official's Son (John 4:46-54)

The situation is one that touches the heart of every parent. Disease and death enter into the home of every man, whether he is a common working man or a distinguished official. All can identify with the anguish in his heart over the critical illness of his

---

Four Things That Make This Miracle of Particular Note

- Opens major portion of Galilean ministry
- Second miracle in Cana
- Performed from a distance
- Performed for a royal official

son. What father would not have determined to do all that he could to save his son from death? Perhaps this man, Jesus, about whom he had heard so much, could heal his son.

The royal official left Capernaum to go to Jesus personally. It would be a long and difficult journey from Capernaum to Cana. Cana was 2,849 feet above sea level, while Capernaum was on the northwest shore of the Sea of Galilee at 682 feet below sea level. The distance between the two cities was approximately twenty miles uphill. When he arrived, he asked the Lord to come with him and heal his son who was at the point of death.

The reply of Jesus seems almost out of character. It appears to indicate a certain degree of impatience on the Lord's part with the urgent appeal of this distraught man for his son. However, the language indicates that Jesus was not rebuking this man, but more likely a multitude that had gathered around. This is not difficult to envision. Multitudes followed Jesus, and now with the arrival of this official and his urgent request, the excitement and curiosity of the crowd would have grown in anxious anticipation of the Lord's response. There appears to have been no weakness in the faith of the royal official, but quite a bit of weakness on the part of the multitude. The statement of Jesus did not deter this distraught father: "Sir, come down before my child dies." What happened next was a mighty test of this man's faith. Jesus said, "Go your way; your son lives."

This man had come with the conviction that if he could reach Jesus in time and persuade Him to come to his home, his son could be saved. He was now being asked to believe that it was not necessary for Jesus to accompany him. "The man believed the word that Jesus spoke to him, and he started off." As he made his way back to Capernaum he was met by his servants with word that his son lived. He had gotten better at the exact hour Jesus had said he would. The man's faith was strengthened, and his whole household believed.

The First Rejection at Nazareth (Luke 4:16-30)

It is very difficult to place all of the events of the early Galilean ministry chronologically. Generally speaking, they are not recorded that way, nor is much emphasis given to the importance of the order in the Scriptures. This study simply presents them in what appears to be a logical progression. The order presented is by no means definitive. Before beginning to examine the first rejection of the Lord at Nazareth, it should be noted that Matthew and Mark record a visit to the city that appears to have taken place at a later time. Some hold that all three accounts are referring to the same visit. There are many similarities in the accounts, but also many differences. The differences seem to indicate that Matthew and Mark refer to a different visit than the one in Luke 4.

During the days of the Lord, Nazareth was an obscure village of less than desirable reputation. As was the custom of Jesus, He went into the synagogue of wherever He was on the Sabbath day. Standing to read, He read from Isaiah 61:1-2. The text He chose demonstrates that the gospel is not only for the rich, the well educated, or those of earthly importance. It is for all. So, in this small village of Nazareth, in the synagogue that Jesus had attended in His youth, He revealed Himself. He chose a passage that presented the Messiah as a minister to the sick and

Outside of Nazareth is a precipice that may have been the place where the Jewish leaders intended to cast down Jesus to His death.

afflicted, a teacher of the neglected, a savior and comforter of the oppressed. With the eyes of the people in the synagogue fastened upon Him, Jesus said, "Today this Scripture has been fulfilled in your hearing."

It is obvious that at first the people did not understand the full import of what Jesus had said, but slowly a smoldering doubt and even scorn begins to be voiced. Jesus heard their words and knew their hearts. To this growing current of anger and unrest, He said, "No doubt you will quote this proverb to me, Physician, heal yourself. Whatever we heard was done in Capernaum, do here in your home town as well." Jesus continued on and addressed their unbelief in a most forceful manner, "No prophet is welcome in his home town."

The Lord than gave two examples. Elijah was sent of God to a Gentile home for shelter, sent to the widow of Sarepta, because she had the faith to share even the last morsel of meal and oil with God's prophet. Elisha, with many Jewish lepers living and dying, helped Naaman, the Syrian, when Naaman demonstrated faith by ultimately obeying the words of the prophet. The implication was that of the Messiah being rejected by His own people but received and honored by the Gentiles. The blessings of God would be poured out upon the Gentiles as the Jews rejected and scorned the Chosen One.

That this was clearly the implication of Jesus' statement is seen by the reaction of those in the synagogue. The normally quiet synagogue became a place of turmoil as they reacted in mob-like fashion. They physically removed the Lord from the synagogue, herded Him through the narrow streets of the little village, intent upon casting Him from the brow of the hill upon which Nazareth was built to His death. They did not succeed, as the passage says, "Passing through their midst, He went His way."

Questions

1. Jesus' message as He travelled through Galilee was: "Repent for the kingdom of heaven is at hand." Define **repentance**._____
   _____
   _____

2. Is **repentance** the same as **godly sorrow**? Explain. _____
   _____
   _____

3. How can we know that the nobleman believed that Jesus could save his son? _____
   _____
   _____

4. Give Bible evidence that shows "the gospel is for all." _____
   _____

5. Explain the Jews' reaction to Jesus' teaching that the gospel was for the Gentiles as well as the Jews. _____
   _____
   _____

6. Jesus said to the nobleman and to those around, "Except ye see signs and wonders ye will in no wise believe." What is the difference between these two parts of a miracle (**signs** and **wonders**)?_____
   _____
   _____

Notes

9 The Calling of the Four Fishermen

(Matt. 4:18-22; Mark 1:16-20; Luke 5:1-11)

This was not the first time that Peter and Andrew, as well as James and John, had seen or been with Jesus. John told us of their earlier time together. John 1 described the meeting, and in chapters 2 through 4 had mentioned the "disciples" of the Lord who had accompanied Him. It appears that, after returning to Galilee with Jesus, these men had scattered to their homes and resumed their occupations. It doesn't appear that any of them had been with Jesus when He experienced His first rejection at Nazareth.

Luke gives the most information about this event. The disciples had spent the whole night unsuccessfully fishing. Early in the morning they had returned and were mending their nets. Multitudes gathered as Jesus taught. Jesus requested the use of Simon's boat because of the people. In the boat, out a little way from the shore, all would be able to see and hear the Lord. After finishing His teaching, Jesus commanded the disciples to go out further and lower their nets. All of this appears most reasonable in order of occurrence, but our emphasis should be on the event itself.

The Sea of Galilee is a lake approximately 7.5 miles wide and 14 miles long.

"Put out into the deep water and let down your nets for a catch" (Luke 5:4). This was the command that Jesus gave to these experienced fishermen when He had finished speaking. Peter demonstrated surprise and faith when he replied, "Master, we worked hard all night and caught nothing, but at your bidding I will let down the nets." Consequently, the catch was so large that the nets were breaking. Their partners in another boat came to help them, and both boats were filled with fish to the point of almost sinking. These men were being asked to leave their businesses and homes in order to follow Jesus. This event had to strengthen their faith.

"Depart from me, for I am a sinful man, O Lord," was Peter's humble confession. It was a natural reaction of a noble and good man who found himself in the presence of deity in a way that he had not before realized. It calls to mind Isaiah 6:5. Surely Peter's statement was actually a fervent appeal that in spite of his human frailty and sinfulness, Jesus would permit him to remain in His company. Jesus responded by saying, "Do not fear, from now on you will be catching men." This great miracle, so contrary to their experience as fishermen, confirmed their faith and enabled Jesus to confirm their call with the promise to make their work that of "catching men." Thus begins a close association with Jesus that no other men but the other apostles would enjoy.

Ministry in Capernaum (Matt. 8:14-17; Mark 1:21-34; Luke 4:31-41)

Having called four of His apostles along the shore of the Sea of Galilee, Jesus entered the city of Capernaum. On the Sabbath day, He went into the synagogue and began to teach the people. Their reaction was one of amazement, for the Lord taught with authority and not as the scribes.

There were several things which caused his teaching to differ from that of the scribes. There was no lack of self-assertion in their teaching; but their words did not carry weight. Their teaching was based chiefly on tradition; it dwelt much on the "mint and anise and cumin" of religion, but neglected "judgment and mercy and faith." Christ's teaching, on the contrary, was eminently spiritual. And then he practiced what he taught. Not so with the scribes (*Pulpit Commentary*, XVI: 5).

In the synagogue that day was a man possessed by the spirit of an unclean demon. The origin and exact nature of demons is not conclusively known, but during the time of Jesus they took possession of certain individuals and often inflicted both physical and mental torment upon them. This demon recognized Jesus and identified Him with a loud voice. Jesus silenced the demon, rebuked him and cast him out of the man. Although the demon threw the man into convulsions and cast him down in the midst of the synagogue, he suffered no lasting effects. As the people left the synagogue, reports of Jesus began to spread all over the region to Galilee.

Upon leaving the synagogue, Jesus went to the house of Simon Peter in Capernaum where He was informed that Peter's mother-in-law was sick with a great fever. Jesus stood over her, rebuked the fever, took her hand and raised her up. She was completely healed and able to show hospitality to them. This was the Sabbath day and the crowds waited until sunset, then they began to bring their sick with them to be healed. Jesus laid His hands on every one of the sick and healed them. Those suffering from demon possession had the demons cast out.

First General Tour of Galilee (Matt. 4:23-25; Mark 1:35-39; Luke 4:42-44)

The gospels tell us that Jesus would often remove himself from the crowds and go to a place where He could have some privacy and pray. Regularly Jesus availed Himself of the comfort, strength, help, and inspiration that communication with His Father provided. Here in the early morning, after such a great day in the city of Capernaum, Jesus sought that help. While He was doing so,

Notes

Simon Peter, an impetuous individual and early in his discipleship, was leading a multitude of people in search of Jesus. While the multitude sought to persuade Jesus to remain in Capernaum, that was not the only city to which He had been sent. Jesus would go to other towns and other cities of Galilee, teaching them the good tidings of the kingdom of God. So He went throughout Galilee teaching in the synagogues, healing the sick and the demon possessed. News of the work of Jesus spread north into Syria, the region just north of Palestine and under Roman rule. Great multitudes came from many different places to follow Jesus. They came from Galilee, Jerusalem, Judaea; even Decapolis.

> Decapolis – The Decapolis was a region southeast of the Sea of Galilee, comprising ten Greek cities, nine east of the Jordan and one (Beth-shan) west. These cities were founded by followers of Alexander the Great, and were reestablished by Pompey (63 B.C.) who hoped to use them to establish Roman rule in Palestine. Pliny, the first writer to mention the Decapolis, lists the original ten cities as Beth-shan (Scythopolis), Pella, Dion, Kanatha, Raphana, Hippos, Gadara, Philadelphia (Rabbath-ammon), Damascus, and Gerasa (Jarash) (*Baker's Bible Atlas*, 192).

Cleansing of a Leper (Matt. 8:2-4; Mark 1:40-45; Luke 5:12-16)

Throughout the cities of Galilee many were healed and the gospel of the kingdom of God was proclaimed. The healing of this leper is a striking example of the healing work of Jesus. What is leprosy?

> A slowly progressing and intractable disease characterized by subcutaneous nodules, scabs or cuticular crusts and white shining spots appearing to be deeper than the skin. Other signs are (1) that of the hairs of the affected part turn white and (2) that later there is a growth of "quick raw flesh." This disease in as especial manner rendered its victims unclean; even contact with a leper defiled whoever touched him, so while the cure of other diseases is called healing, that of leprosy is called cleansing (*The International Bible Encyclopedia*, III: 1867).

This miracle took place in an unnamed city in Galilee and demonstrates the great faith of this man. As he approached Jesus, it was necessary to enter into the city which was contrary to the letter of the Law of Moses (Lev. 13:45-46). He dropped to his knees before Jesus, even falling on his face and offering homage to the Lord, saying simply, "Lord, if you are willing, you can make me clean." Mark tells us that Jesus was moved with compassion, touched the man and cleansed him. Jesus did not break the Law by intentionally touching this leper. He was not defiled by the touch. In fact, He cleansed the one He did touch. He wasn't going to catch or spread the disease. Simply at the words of Jesus the man was cleansed of his leprosy.

Upon cleansing him, Jesus told the man to go to the priest. There are at least two reasons why Jesus gave him that instruction. (1) It was part of the Law of Moses (Lev. 14:1-32). (2) It was for his cleansing. The priests served as health officials and before the leper could become part of regular society again, he had to go to them for inspection. Even though the man was told not to spread the news of his cleansing, he did not obey this command. He had been cleansed of leprosy and was so overjoyed that apparently he could not contain himself, and he began to spread abroad word of what had happened. The reaction was so great that Jesus had difficulty in the cities because of the multitudes that came to hear and be healed. Ultimately the Lord had to resort to uninhabited places and the crowds would come to Him.

Why the command to tell no man? Several different reasons have been suggested. Perhaps it was because of the messianic expectations of the people. They were looking for a messiah who would throw off the yoke of Roman bondage in a military fashion, and Jesus desired to keep such excitement to a minimum. It is also possible that He wanted to allow time to finish His work, thus avoiding the final confrontation with the Jewish leaders.

Questions

1. Explain how Peter, Andrew, James, and John would go from being "fishermen" to "fishers of men." _____
   _____

2. Explain the circumstances that caused Peter to say to Jesus, "Depart from me, for I am a sinful man." _____
   _____

3. How was the teaching of Jesus different from the teaching of the scribes?
   _____
   _____

4. Explain the process Jesus used to rid the man of demons that had taken up residence in his body. _____
   _____

5. Read Isaiah 53:4 and explain how Jesus fulfilled this prophecy with His ministry in Capernaum. _____
   _____

6. As Jesus went about healing the multitudes, why did He request that those healed not tell others about the healing? _____
   _____

7. What was required on the part of those healed by Jesus? (What conditions did they have to meet to make the healing successful?) How does this compare with "faith healings" today? _____
   _____
   _____

10
The Healing of the Paralytic

(Matt. 9:1-8; Mark 2:1-12; Luke 5:17-26)

Jesus had returned to Capernaum, called His city, and was sitting in "the house," probably the home of Simon Peter. The home was filled to capacity, even to the doorway. The streets outside were crowded with people. Some of those listening were Pharisees and teachers of the law from every village of Galilee, Judea, and Jerusalem. It is apparent that the rapid rise in the popularity of Jesus was becoming a concern to the leaders of the Jews. Four individuals came into this crowded situation carrying a man who was paralyzed on a bed. However, they could not get through the crowd so they went to the roof of the house to lower the man into the home. Most of the homes in Palestine were built with flat roofs and many had outside staircases that led to the roof. The roof itself would be composed of tiles that could easily be removed and replaced without damage to the house. Luke makes it clear that this particular house did have a tile roof. So with determination born of faith, they carried out their plan and lowered the sick man into the presence of Jesus. Jesus was impressed and moved by their faith.

It is important to notice that the forgiveness of this man's sins and the healing of his affliction were not synonymous, nor did they take place simultaneously. The most important need this sick man had was not physical. It was forgiveness of his sins. That was first and foremost; the healing could come later. He knew that telling the man that his sins were forgiven in the presence of Pharisees and teachers of the law would cause a very negative reaction. Jesus did not fear controversy or its consequences. What was the controversy? Only God can forgive sins. For Jesus to make such a statement was blasphemy as far as the Pharisees and teachers were concerned. One of the meanings of blasphemy is to "arrogate or claim any attribute, power, or authority which belongs exclusively to God." To accuse Jesus of blasphemy was a very serious charge. Leviticus 24:16 declared death to be the punishment for blasphemy. If Jesus had been a mere man, or even an extraordinary man, the accusation of the Pharisees and teachers of the law would have been correct. But Jesus was the Son of God. His statement was a dramatic and direct claim of deity. It implied supreme authority. Jesus claimed this authority and then demonstrated it by a miracle.

The first evidence of the validity of the Lord's claim was to read their hearts and declare out loud what they were thinking within themselves. He then said that He would prove that He had the power to forgive sins by a miracle. "Which is easier? To say, your sins have been forgiven you, or to say, rise and walk?" Obviously it would be easier to say that the man's sins had been forgiven because there would have been no visible proof one way or the other. But if He commanded the man to rise up, if He healed the dreadful disease that had rendered the man unable to walk, they would be able to test the reality of His authority. Only by the authority of God could either of those things take place. In order to prove to these Jewish leaders that He had the power to forgive sins, He told the man to get up, take his bed, and go home. He was healed immediately. Those who witnessed this event proclaimed that they had seen remarkable things that day, things they had never seen before.

The Call of Matthew (Matt. 9:9-13; Mark 2:13-17; Luke 5:27-32)

After the healing of the paralytic and the controversy with the Pharisees and teachers of the law, another event took place that caused further controversy. Jesus left the house of Peter and walked by the seaside. As He walked, He passed the collection booth of a tax-gatherer, Matthew (Levi, the son of Alphaeus). Tax-gatherers had a profitable occupation, but it was one held in very low esteem. They were considered to be outcasts and even traitors because they assisted Rome in the collection of taxes. In the gospels, tax-gatherers and sinners are often included in the same phrase. Jesus called Matthew to follow Him, and he did. Matthew held a great feast in his home. Many of his colleagues were there, as were Jesus and some of His disciples. This prompted murmuring on the part of the Pharisees and their scribes. They wondered how it was possible for Jesus and His disciples to eat with tax-gatherers and sinners.

The love of Jesus took Him into some of the most unlikely places. His love took Him into the highways and the byways. The Pharisees and their scribes could keep their self-righteous distance from the tax-gatherers, refusing to go into their homes for fear of defiling themselves. They could condemn Jesus for His association with them; but Jesus went right to the heart of the matter.

> "It is not those who are healthy who need a physician, but those who are sick. But go and learn what this means, I desire compassion, and not sacrifice, for I did not come to call the righteous, but sinners."

Jesus was the physician in His statement. The tax-gatherers were the ones who were sick, and the Pharisees and their scribes were the ones who were healthy, the ones who were righteous, at least in their own estimation. They thought they were well but were desperately sick and did not even know it. The tax-gatherers were sick – sick in sin. But to help and to cure them was the very reason Jesus came. The application to all who are self-righteous should be obvious. The charge that Jesus associated with sinners was to His glory, not to His shame. They needed Him. Out of this association came Matthew, the faithful apostle and author of the first gospel. The Pharisees and their scribes did not understand the significance of Hosea 6:6. The ordinances of the Law meant very little if they were not underscored by love and compassion.

Controversy about Fasting (Matt. 9:14-17; Mark 2:18-22; Luke 5:33-39)

John was a man noted for his austere lifestyle; a lifestyle that would have been emulated to a degree by his disciples. It stood in contrast to that of Jesus and His disciples. They partook of the innocent pleasures of life and did in fact eat with tax-gatherers and sinners as a means of taking the gospel to them. This was something that the disciples of John had difficulty understanding. The Pharisees had designated Monday and Thursday as days of fasting, and it is reasonable to believe that John's disciples observed those days as well as others as they sought to imitate the lifestyle of John. Jesus and His disciples did not observe these traditions of men, and the Pharisees and the disciples of John wanted to know why.

Jesus used four illustrations to explain. The first was a wedding, a time of great joy and feasting. At a time such as that, fasting would be inappropriate. Jesus also used the illustration of a person attempting to sew a piece of cloth that was not shrunk on an old garment. When the new patch shrunk, it would rend the old material, thus ruining it. The idea is that it is inappropriate to mix the old with the new. Luke added that the new piece was torn from a new garment, thereby ruining not only the old garment, but the new as well. Thirdly, Jesus spoke of putting new wine in old wineskins. Old wineskins had already expanded as far as they could go. When new wine was placed into them, it would ferment and increase in volume. Already stretched to their limit, the old skins would burst. Lastly, found in Luke's account, old wine was good, the new wine inferior. To drink the old wine and immediately follow it with the new wine was disappointing. It was, in the context, inappropriate to do so.

The lesson of all four illustrations was that things which do not harmonize should not be put together. Fasting was not a part of the gospel of the kingdom of God.

Questions

1. Why would the increasing popularity of Jesus be of concern to the Jewish leaders? _____

   _____

2. Why was the paralytic man forgiven of his sins *before* he was healed?_____

   _____

3. Why was Jesus accused of blasphemy? _____

   _____

4. Explain why most people considered Matthew an unlikely candidate to be chosen by Jesus as one of His apostles. _____

   _____

5. When Jesus was questioned as to why He didn't observe traditional days of fasting, He responded by using four images to explain His reason. Explain what Jesus taught from each of the following:
   a. A wedding _____
   b. A new piece of cloth _____
   c. New wine and old wineskins _____
   d. Old wine and new wine _____

6. Today, under what circumstances is **fasting** wrong? _____

   _____

   When would it be acceptable? Use Scripture to support your answer._____

   _____

11 Controversy at the Pool of Bethesda

(John 5:1-47)

The Galilean ministry was apparently interrupted by a visit to Jerusalem for one of the great feasts of the Jews. It seems reasonable to believe that this was the Passover, the second of four Passovers John mentions in connection with the ministry of the Lord.

(Verses 1-16)

The miracle took place at the Pool of Bethesda, a spring-fed pool of water located southeast of the temple area. Many of the earliest and best manuscripts do not include the last phrase of verse 3 and all of verse 4. A great multitude of sick and crippled people were lying in the five porches surrounding the pool.

The pool of Bethesda as reconstructed in the Model City in the Israel Museum.

Out of all of these people Jesus chose a man who was certainly in a pitiable state, being alone and constantly pushed aside by others as he would try to make his way to the water, and he had been sick for 38 years. It is interesting that Jesus approached this man who did not know who He was. Jesus came into the world to lead men to faith in Him. That was the primary reason for the miracles. The miracles of Jesus and His apostles were faith producing, not faith dependent! The first thing Jesus did for this man was to stir anew in his heart the great desire to be healed and the belief that he could be. When the Lord told him, "Arise, take up your pallet, and walk," he was immediately and completely healed. This miracle did not depend upon the man's faith in Jesus. He did not know who the Lord was. Later, when the man was being persecuted by the Jewish leaders for carrying his pallet on the Sabbath day, Jesus revealed Himself to him more fully. He had made his body whole, now He sought to give him the more needed spiritual health as well, telling him to sin no more. The man informed the Jews that it was Jesus who had made him well.

This second visit of Jesus to Jerusalem created a great furor. The manner and the time of this miracle caused heated discussion. Jesus healed this man on the Sabbath day, knowing that it would cause bitter criticism against Him. He made a deliberate choice concerning the man and the time. He approached the man. He told him to take up his pallet and walk, knowing that the sight of a man carrying such a burden through the Sabbath Day crowds would create controversy. When they knew that it had been Jesus who had healed the man, the attitude of the Jewish leaders turned ugly. The stage was set for the first lengthy recorded public discourse of Jesus. It arose in defense against the charge that He was a Sabbath breaker (a crime punishable by death – Lev. 23:29-30 and Num. 15:32-36), but it quickly merged into the larger claim that He was the Son of God.

(Verses 17-29)

Jesus did not defend His actions by attacking the traditions of the Jews concerning the Sabbath, traditions they had allowed to supersede the Scriptures. Jesus based His defense upon His unity and equality with God. He declared His own authority over the Sabbath, as absolute as God Himself. The Jewish leaders understood immediately that the declarations of Jesus were implicit and explicit claims to deity. The Lord made it clear that He was subject to the Father, but was His very Son and acting in conjunction with Him. Jesus taught that those who did not honor Him were not honoring the Father. How they reacted to Him, the Son of Man, would determine their fate in judgment.

(Verses 30-47)

Jesus gave five witnesses that attested to His identity. First was Himself, but it was not a witness given independently of the Father. The second witness was John the Baptist. Jesus pointed out that John's testimony was known to all. The third witness was even greater than John. It was the miracles Jesus performed. They stood as evidence of the direct work of God through Him. Even the scholarly Nicodemus had understood this to be true when he said to Jesus in John 3:2, "Rabbi, we know that you have come from God as a teacher; for no one can do these signs that you do unless God is with him." In the miracles the fourth witness was found – God the Father. The testimony was found in the ability of Jesus to perform these mighty works. The fifth witness was the scriptures. The testimony of the Old Testament was powerful and clear. His coming was the primary theme of the Old Testament, but they would not believe. Now the battle lines are clearly drawn. The Sabbath controversy would continue to rage. The leaders of the Jews began to plot to put Him to death. Approximately two years later, Jesus would die on the cross.

Controversy (Matt. 12:1-8; Mark 2:23-28; Luke 6:1-5)

The Sabbath controversy did not remain in Jerusalem. It continued in Galilee. On another Sabbath Day, Jesus and His disciples were walking on the roads leading them through ripened fields of grain. Deuteronomy 23:24-25 was understood to mean that the hungry were permitted to take any grain they could reach from the highway to satisfy their hunger; they were not permitted to enter the field itself. The Pharisees charged the Lord's disciples with breaking the Sabbath. They charged them with reaping, threshing and winnowing as they plucked the grain, rubbed it out in their hands, and blew the chaff away. Jesus offered five arguments to show the fallacy of their charges.

First, He referred to an event in the life of David. There was no attempt by Jesus to discuss the propriety of what David did when he sought food for himself and his hungry men while in flight from Saul. The only food available was the shewbread, which the Law of Moses strictly forbade anyone to eat other than the priests (Lev. 24:5-9). Since they accepted David in spite of what he did, why criticize the disciples? The second argument indicated that there were certain inevitable conflicts of duty arising from the Law that God had left man to work out according to his own conscience. The Law prohibited any work on the Sabbath, yet also commanded certain sacrifices to be offered in the temple. When the sacrifices came on a Sabbath, the priests offered them. Why criticize His disciples when they did not criticize the priests for apparently breaking the Law? He concluded this argument with a majestic declaration, "Something greater than the temple is here." The third argument was from a statement found in Hosea 6:6. This was a Hebraism meaning, "I desire not only sacrifice, but also mercy." This argument embraces the fourth as well, "The Sabbath was made for man, and not man for the Sabbath." The Lord's point was that His disciples were without guilt in this matter and the Pharisees would have recognized that fact if they had understood Hosea's words. Jesus' final argument was a clear declaration of His personal authority, "The Son of Man is Lord even of the Sabbath."

> Even as Jesus proclaimed himself greater than the temple, so he declares himself Lord of the Sabbath. This is a clear declaration of his deity. The temple and the Sabbath were the two central features of the Old Testament law. Jesus transcends the O.T. Law. He does not here abrogate the law, but claims authority over it and relates it to the great principles of mercy and love. He later set it aside when he died on the cross and gave at Pentecost God's final plan of salvation (Foster, R.C. Gospel Studies, II: 34).

Jesus often referred to Himself as the Son of Man – over 30 times in Matthew, 15 times in Mark, 25 times in Luke, and 12 times in John. It is frequently found in the Old Testament in the book of Psalms; Daniel and Ezekiel use it over 90 times referring to Himself and His prophetic ministry. To be extremely simple, it appears that Jesus used this phrase because it is so messianic and because of the connection it gave Him with all men.

Notes

(lined note-taking area)

Questions

1. Why were the Jews so angry at Jesus for his healing the man at the Pool of Bethesda? _____
_____

2. What was Jesus' attitude toward the Old Law? _____
_____

3. When the Jews rebuked the Lord's disciples for taking the grain from around the fields on the Sabbath, Jesus used several past events to answer their argument. Briefly explain each of the following:
   a. David and the shew bread (Lev. 24: 5-9) _____
   _____

   b. Conflicts of duty _____
   _____

   c. Hosea 6:6 _____
   _____

   d. "Sabbath was made for man, not the man for Sabbath." _____
   _____

4. What was the primary reason for Jesus' miracles? _____
   a. To end the world of disease
   b. To destroy the Old Law
   c. To help men to believe in Him
   d. To confront the Jews' false teaching

5. Why did Jesus **not** heal all of the sick and crippled around the Pool of Bethesda? _____
   a. He did not have the time.
   b. Many lacked the faith necessary to be healed.
   c. He feared the Jews would retaliate.
   d. His mission was not about physical healing.

6. In what sense was Jesus "the son of God"? _____
   _____
   _____

7. In what sense was Jesus "the son of man"? _____
   _____
   _____

8. List **four** circumstances that confirm the deity of Christ.
   _____
   _____
   _____
   _____

Jesus: The Bread of Life

12 The Man with the Withered Hand and More Controversy

(Matt. 12:9-14; Mark 3:1-6; Luke 6:6-11)

The combined accounts of Matthew, Mark, and Luke give us a clear picture of what happened as Jesus entered into a synagogue on another Sabbath. In the synagogue was a man with a withered hand. The scribes and Pharisees were watching Jesus very carefully, even asking Him a question to ensnare Him. What would Jesus do? He commanded the man with the withered hand to stand forth and stretch his hand out, focusing all attention on the critical issue of whether it was lawful to do good on the Sabbath or to do harm, to save a life or to kill. The Lord healed the man on the Sabbath day in the synagogue where all could see. He helped the man and exposed the hypocrisy of the Pharisees at the same time. His illustration of the sheep in the pit showed that the Pharisees had more mercy concerning an animal in distress on the Sabbath than they did for a fellow human being in need.

The Lord's question concerning doing good or evil on the Sabbath, healing or killing, was not answered by the Pharisees, and Jesus knew that their silence was caused by the hardness of their hearts. The Pharisees objected to Jesus healing this man on the Sabbath, but they were spending a portion of the day plotting to kill Him. It is interesting that Mark tells us that, after this event, the Pharisees left the synagogue and took counsel with the Herodians about how they might destroy Jesus. The Herodians were a powerful political party devoted to the interests of the Herod family. As such, they were enemies of the Pharisees. However, their common hatred of Jesus caused them to join forces to destroy Him.

Jesus and the Multitudes (Matt. 12:15-21)

Jesus was aware of the plotting being done by the Pharisees and Herodians, and as He left the synagogue great multitudes followed Him. Jesus taught them and healed the sick. The quotation from Isaiah 42 gives a beautiful picture of the mercy the Messiah would bring to the sinful, the sick, the suffering, and the downtrodden. "A battered reed" suggests a man oppressed by sin or misfortune that Jesus will not destroy as he seeks forgiveness and help. A "smoldering wick" is the wick of a lamp which is about to flicker out for lack of oil or perhaps because of an imperfection of the wick itself. The light is feeble and annoying, but Jesus would not snuff it out. He will fan it to flame again. He was a man of mercy, comfortable with the common man and they with Him.

The Selection of the Twelve Apostles (Mark 3:13-19; Luke 6:12-16)

Jesus often went to His Father in prayer. The night before He chose His twelve apostles was one such time. It was evidently on a mountain somewhere near Capernaum that this momentous event took place. Of His disciples, Jesus selected twelve to be His apostles. The word apostle means "one who is sent." It was a fitting title for these twelve men. They were sent forth in a special way to preach the gospel. They were to be special ambassadors of the Lord. The names of the men were Peter, James (son of Zebedee), John, Andrew, Philip, Bartholomew (possibly Nathanael), Matthew, Thomas, James (son of Alphaeus), Thaddaeus (called Judas son of James by Luke), Simon the Zealot, and Judas Iscariot. Matthias would later be added to replace Judas Iscariot, and Paul was specially called to be an apostle. Altogether there were fourteen apostles, but these twelve originally. There is significance to Simon being called Peter, and James and John called Boanerges. Peter means "rock," although not an immovable object; it simply speaks of his character. Boanerges means "sons of thunder."

Begin the Sermon on the Mount (Matt. 5:1-8:1; Luke 6:17-49)

It is my belief that Matthew and Luke describe the same occasion. In Matthew 5:1, Jesus went up into the mountain. We know that He spent the night in prayer to His Father and then chose the apostles. Luke informs us that Jesus came down the next day to a level place with His apostles, and a great multitude of people from various places were there. At this time Jesus delivered the Sermon on the Mount. In this study, it will be approached topically, beginning with the Beatitudes.

The Beatitudes (Matt. 5:3-12; Luke 6:20-26)

"Blessed are the poor in spirit, for theirs is the kingdom of heaven." Luke says, "Blessed are you who are poor, for yours is the kingdom of God." The word "poor" is not describing what a man has, it is describing what a man is. The point that Jesus was making is this: man must come to feel his total depen-

From this photograph from the Sea of Galilee, one can see why the Sermon Jesus preached might be called either the Sermon on the Mount or the Sermon on the Plain.

dence upon God rather than himself. He must come to recognize that he is spiritually destitute, utterly helpless, without God.

"Blessed are those who mourn, for they shall be comforted." This refers to those who mourn over the lost condition of their souls. It describes an individual with a broken heart, broken because of the realization of his sin. To such a one, comfort is promised. In contrast to those who mourn over their soul's condition is the statement found in Luke 6:25, "Woe to you who are well-fed now, for you shall be hungry. Woe to you who laugh now, for you shall mourn and weep." These are the ones with no realization of their soul's condition. They have no godly sorrow brought about by their sins. They delight in the things of the world now, oblivious to their true spiritual state, but eventually they will mourn and weep. For them there will be no comfort.

"Blessed are the gentle, for they shall inherit the earth." Gentle, or meek, describes a condition of the mind and heart. It is an inward virtue. Those who possess it do not show resentment or threaten when they are wronged. It is an evenness of spirit. It is the opposite of bitterness and violence. Jesus said that those who had such a disposition would inherit the earth. "Inherit the earth" is a proverbial expression used to suggest great blessings. The Lord was saying that those who were gentle would be in His kingdom and would receive God's blessings here and now, as well as in the future heavenly land of Promise.

"Blessed are those who hunger and thirst for righteousness, for they shall be satisfied." To paraphrase that, "Blessed are those who vehemently desire to be right before God, for they will obtain it." Hungering and thirsting after righteousness shows that a man must want to come, he must desire it and need it as strongly as he does nourishment for his body. When a person reaches that state, Jesus says that he will be satisfied.

"Blessed are the merciful, for they shall receive mercy." Jesus attached a great, and often over-looked, significance to mercy. Frequently He referred to Hosea 6:6. Many of the Jewish leaders during the time of Christ were without mercy. The Roman world, in which Jesus lived, was extremely lacking in mercy, particularly to slaves and unwanted children. Against this kind of backdrop, Jesus taught the need for mercy. The Lord said that the merciful would receive mercy. That is a basic principle. If we want God to be merciful to us, we must be merciful to others.

"Blessed are the pure in heart, for they shall see God." To be "pure in heart" is to have a singleness of mind, honesty with no hidden motives, no selfish interest; to be true and open in all things. All that we know of the Lord's will for us we know through the Word. Those who know and love the truth, who follow it with a singleness of mind with no ulterior motive, are the "pure in heart." To "see God" means to have a relationship with Him, both on earth and ultimately in heaven.

"Blessed are the peacemakers, for they shall be called sons of God." Jesus was not speaking of one who settles disagreements among men. He was talking about peacemakers who preach the gospel of peace and show men the way back to God. When a man sins, he separates himself from God. There is a need for a restoration. That is the function of the peacemaker. He preaches the gospel of peace and thereby helps to reconcile the sinner to God.

"Blessed are those who have been persecuted for the sake of righteousness, for theirs is the kingdom of heaven." To be a follower of Jesus would not be easy. There would be persecution of all forms, including insults and false charges because of one's adherence to the doctrine of Christ. For those who stood firm no matter what, there would be strength to endure now and eternity in heaven.

Questions

1. How did the Lord use the image of a sheep in the pit to demonstrate the hypocrisy if the Jews? _____

_____

2. Who were the Herodians? _____

_____

3. After a night of prayer, Jesus chose His apostles from among His followers. Match the apostle with his brief description below.

_____ Peter	a. Probably Nathaniel
_____ Andrew	b. The beloved one
_____ James	c. Means "the rock"
_____ John	d. Son of Zebedee
_____ Philip	e. Fisherman
_____ Bartholomew	f. Brought Nathaniel to Jesus
_____ Matthew	g. Also called Judas
_____ Thomas	h. Tax collector
_____ James	i. Also called Didymus
_____ Thaddeus	j. Also called the Canaanite
_____ Simon	k. Called "the Less"
_____ Judas	l. Betrayed Jesus

4. What does "Beatitude" mean? _____

_____

5. Explain how the "kingdom of heaven" belongs to the "poor in spirit"? _____

_____

6. What kind of comfort awaits those who mourn for their sinful condition?

_____

7. Give a synonym for "gentle." How do the "gentle inherit the earth"? _____

_____

8. Describe the behavior of one who "hungers and thirsts for righteousness."

_____

_____

9. Give a synonym for "merciful." Explain Hosea 6:6 in light of this beatitude.

_____

_____

10. Explain how the kingdom of heaven belongs to those who are "persecuted for righteousness' sake." _____

_____

11. A person who is "pure in heart" is a person who _____

_____.

12. Give evidence that the Pharisees were steeped in hypocrisy? _____

_____

_____

13

Continuing the Sermon on the Mount

(Matt. 5:1-8:1, Luke 6:17-49)

The Salt of the Earth (Matt. 5:13-16)

Jesus addressed the need for God's people to be useful in His service and their responsibility to influence others for good. There are at least four important characteristics of salt that should be considered. First, salt suggests purity. To the Romans, salt was the purest of all substances. Second, salt preserves, it keeps things from corrupting. In the ancient world it was the most common of preservatives. To be a follower of Jesus a person must keep from corruption and have a preserving effect upon those with whom he comes into contact. Third, salt seasons. Being a follower of Christ is to life what salt is to food. Life without Christ has no real flavor. Fourth, salt promotes thirst. A follower of Jesus must live in such a way as to stimulate thirst in others for the Lord. When salt loses these, and other, properties and can no longer perform its functions, it is useless and should be cast out. A Christian who has ceased to perform his functions has become useless in the kingdom as well.

Light dispels darkness. That is the same function that a follower of Christ performs as he reflects the light of Christ in the darkness of the world. Light that is hidden is useless. So too is a follower of Jesus who hides that fact. A Christian's responsibility is to be useful in service to God – to exercise influence for good.

The Law and the Prophets (Matt. 5:17-20)

Jesus lived His life while the Law of Moses was in effect. He taught many things that were not specifically set forth in that Law as He was preparing the way for the "law of faith," the "perfect law of liberty" (Rom. 3:27; James 1:25). He often exposed the fallacy of some of the traditional interpretations of the Law. This led to charges that He advocated breaking the Law of Moses or doing away with it. Jesus taught that the Jews were to respect and obey the Law but that they were to understand it correctly. The Lord did not come to destroy the Law, but to fulfill it; to bring it to fruition and completion. Until He had completed that work, not even the smallest letter of the Hebrew alphabet, the jot, or even the smallest part of a letter, the tittle, would pass from it. Obedience to that Law was essential for the Jews to be saved at that time. Failure to obey it, or to teach others not to obey it, would result in condemnation. But it had to be properly understood. Obedience had to come from the proper motive or it was useless. A follower of the Lord had to exceed the shallow righteousness of the scribes and Pharisees.

Anger (Matt. 5:21-26)

Jesus referred to the sixth commandment (Ex. 20:13), and then showed that even the initial stages of unjust anger leading to such an act are wrong. Unjust anger places a person in danger of an earthly court. If it progresses to name-calling, such as Raca, meaning stupid or empty-headed, the person would be in danger of the supreme court. If it continues to progress to the point of calling someone a fool, implying that he is morally worthless, the person stands in danger of the fiery hell. The Law taught that the act of murder was wrong. Jesus showed that the inward feelings leading to such an act are wicked as well.

The Lord taught that in wrongs committed among brethren, the wrong-doer has the God-given responsibility to face the one he has wronged and rectify the situation. So serious was the responsibility that even if the wrong-doer was in the midst of making an offering to God, he was to stop and make the situation right first. Jesus used the metaphor of the civil court as He continued to teach about sins against others. The "opponent" was the one sinned against. Jesus illustrated the seriousness of failure to reconcile quickly by indicating that it would place one in danger of divine judgment without mercy.

Lust (Matt. 5:27-30)

Jesus introduced the subject of lust. He was not talking about the passing thought of sexual desire through the mind. Jesus was talking about gazing upon someone, letting the mind linger and build lust toward another individual. That is as wrong as the act itself. It is not the act itself but equally sinful. To illustrate the seriousness of such a sin, Jesus referred to an eye and a hand. Better to lose such a valuable organ than to permit it to contribute to the loss of one's soul.

Divorce and Remarriage (5:31-32)

This Pharasaic tradition which the Lord cites is based on a distortion of Deuteronomy 24:1-4. The meaning of these verses has been hotly disputed among the rabbinical schools. Shammai, insisting on a criminal and legal cause for the divorce, emphasized the word "some unseemly thing," and limited it to adultery. Hillel stressed the words "find no favor in his eyes," and allowed divorce for anything displeasing to the husband. Rabbi Akiba went even further, permitting divorce if a man simply found a more appealing woman. For other information available to us in the New Testament, it is evident that the Pharisees shared the very loose views of Hillel if not worse ones (Matt. 19:3, 7), and were far less concerned about the reason for the divorce and its unholy consequences on the victim than for the following of proper forms. Their obsession with legal niceties to the complete disregard of moral principle is again revealed. The Pharisees viewed divorce as a right, and saw the words of Moses as a command (Matt. 19:7), rather than a permissive allowance. By so doing they had wholly misapprehended the law and its purpose. God's attitude toward divorce had been made abundantly clear in the Old Testament whose canon had virtually closed with the ringing words, "I hate putting away, saith Jehovah, the God of Israel" (Mal. 2:16). Consistent with that divine sentiment the words of Deuteronomy 24:1-4 were intended to put a check on already rampant divorce, not to introduce and encourage it. Jesus describes the teaching of the law on divorce as a concession to Israel's "hardness of heart" (Matt. 19:8); not surely a "hardness" of stubborn rebellion, which would have been intolerable (Heb. 3:7-11), but one borne of spiritual backwardness (Mk. 6:52) (Earnhart, *Christianity Magazine*, April 1985).

Jesus' teaching concerning divorce is that fornication on the part of one of the marriage partners is the allowable reason. The one put away for fornication cannot marry another.

Oaths (Matt. 5:33-37)

While the exact wording of the traditional teaching Jesus mentions is not found in the Old Testament, it is possible that He was giving a summation of what the Law taught concerning oaths in such passages as Leviticus 19:12. The problem was in the application of the Law. Apparently the scribes and Pharisees saw the teaching of the Law about oaths as permission to be less than truthful when not under an oath. The evil Jesus addressed was not the taking of oaths, but lying and deception. Jesus made the point that there was nothing by which a person may swear, be it heaven or earth, Jerusalem, or even their own heads, that was not ultimately tied to God and His power. The simple truth was that every word a follower of the Lord utters, whether under oath or not, is before God and must be the truth.

Revenge and Forgiveness (Matt. 5:38-48; Luke 6:27-30, 32-36)

"An eye for an eye, and a tooth for a tooth" expresses the idea that the penalty should match the offense (Deut. 19:18-21). Under the Law this was carried out as a legal act, not as a matter of personal retaliation. Jesus was teaching that our personal lives must be guided by love, restraint, forgiveness; not by vengeance, retaliation, and hatred. His followers should be of the mind to allow themselves to be oppressed rather than to be the oppressors. The traditional teaching of "love your neighbor, and hate your enemy" was probably arrived at due to the nature of some of the imprecatory psalms, such as Psalm 109, but it was not a valid interpretation of the Old Law. By saying "love your enemies," He was speaking of a love that does not find its origin on earth. Man does not normally act that way, but God does. He has consistently loved His enemies, and that divine love has nothing to do with some sort of attractive quality found in man. The book of Ecclesiastes, in chapter 7:20, makes it clear that what mankind has succeeded in doing is making itself, almost to a person, morally repugnant. Yet God loves us. He loves the unloving (Rom. 5:8). Followers of Christ must strive for that kind of love.

Notes

Notes

_____
_____
_____
_____
_____
_____
_____
_____
_____
_____
_____
_____
_____
_____
_____
_____
_____
_____
_____
_____
_____
_____
_____
_____
_____
_____
_____
_____
_____
_____
_____
_____
_____
_____
_____

Questions

1. Give ways that a Christian is compared to "salt." _____
    _____
    _____

2. THE LAW of MOSES vs. THE GOSPEL of JESUS CHRIST
    a. The Law of Moses said "Thou shall not kill." Jesus taught that _____
        _____
        _____

    b. The Law of Moses said "Thou shall not commit adultery." Jesus taught
        _____
        _____

    c. Read Deuteronomy 24: 1-4. Contrast the Law of Moses and Christ's law
        concerning **divorce**. _____
        _____
        _____

3. What did Christ teach about **lying and deception**? _____
    _____
    _____

4. Discuss **retaliation** in both the Old Law and in the gospel of Jesus Christ.
    _____
    _____